Empire of Algorithms

Empire of Algorithms

How AI is Redrawing the Map of Power Among Nations

By

Arden Hale

Vij Books

New Delhi (India)

Published by

Vij Books
(Publishers, Distributors & Importers)
4836/24, 3rd Floor, Ansari Road
Delhi – 110 002
Phone: 91-11-43596460
Mobile: 98110 94883
e-mail: contact@vijpublishing.com
www.vijbooks.in

ISBN: 978-93-90349-43-2 (HB)

ISBN: 978-93-90349-33-3 (PB)

This book was developed using advanced writing tools to support the drafting and ideation process. All content has been thoughtfully curated, refined, and reviewed to ensure quality and relevance.

Contents

Introduction

When Code Becomes Sovereignty

The modern world is being reordered by something that cannot be seen, weighed, or touched. It is not a new territory claimed, a weapon unveiled, or a currency struck. It is a pattern of logic expressed in lines of code, fed by oceans of data, and executed by machines whose operations increasingly escape the grasp of human supervision. Artificial intelligence is not simply another tool in humanity's technological repertoire; it is becoming the organising principle of global power. Just as gunpowder redrew medieval maps, and nuclear weapons recalibrated twentieth-century strategy, AI now reshapes the balance of nations, corporations, and individuals. The frontier of power has shifted: sovereignty itself is being rewritten in code.

What makes AI unlike previous revolutions is not only its scope but its structure. Steam engines and electricity extended human physical capacity; radio and the internet expanded communication. All transformed societies, yet none rewired the very mechanisms by which authority, wealth, and legitimacy are exercised at planetary scale. AI does not merely assist in production or communication; it decides, recommends, predicts, and governs. It creates asymmetries that multiply across every domain—military, financial, political, and cultural. The consequences are not incremental but systemic: advantage compounds, and the gap between those who command AI and those who must submit to it widens inexorably.

This book sets out to examine artificial intelligence as the atomic bomb of geopolitics—a comparison not made for sensational effect but to highlight a structural truth. Nuclear weapons redefined what it meant to be a superpower. They imposed a new architecture of deterrence, one in which existential threat underpinned the global order. AI, by contrast, confers a quieter but no less decisive kind of leverage. Its arsenal is invisible: stockpiles of data, vast computational infrastructures, networks of engineers and scientists. Its deployment is not measured in detonations but in shifts of dependency—nations finding their financial systems exposed to algorithmic crashes, their citizens profiled and predicted by foreign technologies, their militaries reliant on sensors and code they cannot control.

What distinguishes AI from other forms of power is that it erodes the line between civilian and military, public and private, national and global. A semiconductor factory in Taiwan, a server farm in Oregon, a mobile app in Nairobi—all belong to the same geopolitical chessboard. Algorithms cross borders with ease; their influence is unconfined by geography, their effects instantaneous. This universality means that AI is not simply a new weapon or a novel resource, but a structure of empire-building in its own right. The question is no longer who owns territory or oil fields, but who controls the architectures of code that mediate daily life and strategic choice alike.

To grasp the stakes, we must consider how empires have always been built. Fire gave humans supremacy over animals; gunpowder extended dominion over rivals; nuclear fission secured deterrence through annihilation. Each epoch was defined by the technology that shifted the terms of survival and control. AI is the next decisive leap, yet unlike fire or fission, its potency does not depend on dramatic spectacle. Its revolutions occur in silence—an investment algorithm making billions vanish in milliseconds, a predictive policing system entrenching bias across generations, a drone guided to its target not by human judgement but by machine inference. The new frontier of power is one in which influence is exercised not through visible conquest but through invisible coordination of systems.

This invisible arsenal reshapes the calculus of fear itself. During the Cold War, deterrence was embodied in mushroom clouds, the horror of instant annihilation. Today the fear lies in dependency: reliance on a foreign cloud infrastructure, an imported chip, an opaque algorithm controlling borders or financial flows. The deterrence of tomorrow may not be a threat to destroy, but the threat to withhold—to deny access to code, compute, or data. This form of coercion is subtler, yet it carries the same power to determine destinies.

The stakes are not evenly distributed. Just as oil deposits or fertile lands favoured some nations in the past, the new raw material of power—data—is concentrated, extracted, and weaponised unevenly. Populous states generate more data; surveillance regimes collect it more aggressively. Corporations harvest it across borders with little oversight, replicating patterns of colonial extraction. The result is a new form of dependency: smaller nations increasingly reliant on systems designed, owned, and governed elsewhere. Efforts at resistance—data localisation laws, privacy regulations—are important but partial. The gravitational pull of algorithmic empires is strong, and the capacity to resist often depends on resources only the most powerful possess.

Compute—the ability to process data at scale—is the new arms race. The world's most advanced semiconductor fabs are no longer just industrial assets but geostrategic prizes. Cloud infrastructures, controlled by a handful of corporations, function as the digital equivalent of shipping lanes and steel mills, commanding not only commerce but governance. Those with access to high-performance compute can shape the future of medicine, warfare, and governance; those without are left to consume what others create. The hierarchy of nations is thus increasingly a hierarchy of computation.

At the same time, AI is transforming the battlefield of information. Disinformation campaigns once required newspapers, radio broadcasts, or labour-intensive propaganda operations. Now a few lines of code can generate convincing fabrications at scale—deepfakes, automated troll armies, sentiment manipulation—destabilising democracies and reinforcing authoritarian regimes. The power to shape reality itself is being weaponised. The most destabilising wars may not be fought with bombs or missiles but with manipulated truths that corrode trust, leaving societies unable to distinguish fact from fabrication.

Governments are not immune to the temptations of algorithmic governance. From predictive policing to automated welfare systems, states adopt AI in the pursuit of efficiency, risk management, and control. Yet each reliance deepens vulnerability. What happens when the legitimacy of governance rests on black-box systems that cannot be explained or contested? What happens when borders are controlled by algorithms that misclassify, or healthcare allocation depends on models trained on biased data? The fragility of democratic oversight is tested when efficiency becomes the justification for opacity.

The private sector compounds this shift. Technology giants, once seen as service providers, now resemble shadow states. They negotiate with governments, influence international agreements, and provide capabilities once monopolised by militaries. Some develop autonomous weapons, others manage infrastructures critical to national security. In many cases, national sovereignty is effectively outsourced to shareholder-driven entities whose priorities may not align with those of the public. Diplomacy itself is being shaped by corporate architectures of AI.

Yet the empire of algorithms is not solely defined by superpower rivalry or corporate dominance. It is also cultural. Code carries values. The assumption that algorithms are neutral is a myth; they encode hierarchies, preferences, and biases drawn from their creators. As AI spreads globally, so too do the cultural assumptions embedded in its architecture. Will the future be shaped by Western individualism, Chinese collectivism, or an emerging synthesis? Resistance emerges not only through legislation but through culture—movements that seek to preserve pluralism against algorithmic homogenisation, to ensure that digital futures reflect local identities rather than erasing them.

The contest over AI is already the new Great Game of geopolitics. The United States and China vie for supremacy, investing heavily in research, talent, and infrastructure. Middle powers like India, Israel, and South Korea manoeuvre for influence, while Africa and Latin America struggle to avoid becoming permanent data colonies. The spectre of a fragmented internet looms: incompatible standards, competing spheres of influence, divergent technological ecosystems. The dream of a universal digital commons fades, replaced by the possibility of splintered empires of code.

This raises profound questions of human agency. If the infrastructure of daily life—from news feeds to financial systems—is increasingly governed by algorithms, what space remains for individual choice? If the terms of political order are set not in parliaments but in proprietary models, how do citizens retain sovereignty? The narrowing of choice, the shrinking of agency, is one of the most profound transformations AI imposes. Yet resistance is not absent. Activists, technologists, and policymakers work to demand transparency, accountability, and the preservation of human values in the loop. The future of democracy may depend on their success.

History teaches us that transformative technologies are rarely governed effectively in their early decades. The nuclear age was marked by reckless tests, near-misses, and improvised doctrines before stabilising under arms control regimes. With AI, the challenge is more complex. Unlike uranium, code cannot be stockpiled or contained in silos; it proliferates invisibly, replicated at near-zero cost. Regulating it requires not just treaties but an entirely new architecture of governance—one capable of transcending national interests while preserving sovereignty. Whether such an architecture can be built is uncertain.

This book does not offer easy optimism or apocalyptic despair. Instead, it aims to situate artificial intelligence within the long arc of empire-building, showing how power is being reorganised at every level—from individuals to nations to corporations. It asks readers to see AI not only as a set of technologies but as a determinant of sovereignty itself. Who will prosper, who will be dependent, who will govern, and who will be governed—these are the stakes of the algorithmic age.

The chapters ahead trace this transformation in depth: from the algorithmic bomb that redefines power without detonation, to the extraction of data as the new colonial resource; from the geopolitics of compute to the weaponisation of influence; from the rise of algorithmic states to the shadow empires of corporations; from cultural blind spots to the rivalries shaping the twenty-first century. The book concludes with an exploration of possible futures, acknowledging both the fragility of governance and the resilience of human agency.

We are entering a world where sovereignty is coded, where empires are built not with armies but with algorithms, and where survival depends not only on weapons or wealth but on the capacity to command the infrastructures of intelligence itself. To understand this world is to grasp not just a technological revolution, but the reshaping of order, authority, and destiny. This book invites you into that understanding.

Chapter 1

The Algorithmic Bomb

The story of human civilisation can be told through the technologies that shifted the balance of power so dramatically that nothing afterwards could be the same. Fire gave early humans dominion over nature itself, transforming survival into mastery and enabling communities to thrive where they would otherwise perish. Millennia later, gunpowder revolutionised warfare, turning the fortified castles of kings into fragile relics and allowing empires to expand their reach across continents. In the twentieth century, nuclear fission brought about a weapon whose destructive potential was so absolute that it forced the invention of a new kind of politics: deterrence, diplomacy, and doctrines of mutually assured destruction. Each of these breakthroughs marked a threshold moment—a leap from one order of power to another, with consequences that were global and irreversible. Today, artificial intelligence occupies that same historical inflection point. But unlike fire, gunpowder, or the atomic bomb, AI does not announce its power with flames, thunder, or shockwaves. Its influence is quieter, often invisible, yet no less transformative. It is, in many ways, the most consequential force multiplier humanity has ever created.

To call AI an *algorithmic bomb* is not to indulge in metaphor for the sake of drama. It is to recognise that AI represents a decisive leap in asymmetric power—capable of magnifying the capabilities of those who wield it while leaving others increasingly vulnerable. Unlike the atomic bomb, its destructive potential does not lie in singular moments of detonation. Rather, it lies in the cumulative reconfiguration of systems—financial, military, social, and political—through processes so integrated into daily life that they appear almost mundane. In fact, this mundanity is part of its danger. Where nuclear explosions broadcast unmistakable devastation, AI reshapes the world in increments, beneath thresholds of perception, until entire structures of authority and dependency are rewritten.

Consider the financial markets. In May 2010, the so-called "Flash Crash" erased nearly a trillion dollars in market value in less than half an hour, triggered not by malicious actors or geopolitical events, but by high-frequency trading algorithms interacting at speeds beyond human comprehension. The losses were quickly corrected, but the event revealed a profound truth: the stability of global markets—pillars of national wealth and policy—is now contingent on code that can destabilise in ways no regulator can anticipate in real time. This was not a detonation in the conventional sense, but a systemic shock demonstrating how power can be wielded without physical destruction. A single misaligned algorithm can move more capital in minutes than centuries of mercantile trade.

In the realm of policing and security, predictive algorithms are already shaping decisions about who is stopped, searched, or surveilled. Far from being neutral tools, they perpetuate and entrench social biases, but more significantly for geopolitics, they illustrate how states outsource decisions about authority to opaque systems. A city's algorithm may not topple governments, but when multiplied across hundreds of jurisdictions, it shifts how legitimacy is exercised and how populations experience governance. Similarly, in military operations, drone warfare increasingly depends not on the skill of pilots but on target-identification algorithms. These systems can determine life and death in theatres of conflict, yet their functioning often lies beyond the scrutiny of those who deploy them. Power without detonation is power that rewrites the rules of sovereignty.

The concept of stockpiling itself has changed. In the twentieth century, the strength of a nation was measured by how many missiles, tanks, or warheads it could amass. Today, the decisive stockpiles are less visible: petabytes of data, high-performance computing capacity, and concentrations of human talent in machine learning research. The United States, China, and a handful of corporations now hoard these resources with the same zeal once reserved for uranium enrichment. Unlike physical weapons, these stockpiles are cumulative and compounding. Data feeds algorithms, algorithms create competitive advantage, which in turn generates more data. Compute capacity accelerates innovation, reinforcing the lead of those who already possess it. Talent clusters attract more investment and opportunity, further widening the gap. The arsenal of the twenty-first century is therefore not stored in silos or bunkers but in server farms, chip factories, and research labs.

This reconfiguration of stockpiles leads to a new psychology of fear. During the Cold War, fear was visceral: the image of mushroom clouds, the prospect of instant annihilation. Nuclear deterrence depended on this shared horror, the knowledge that an attack would invite retaliation so catastrophic that no rational actor could risk it. With AI, fear operates differently. It is not about annihilation but dependency. What if a nation's financial infrastructure is tied to algorithms controlled abroad? What if a military's logistics rely on semiconductors manufactured in contested territories? What if social cohesion depends on recommendation engines designed by corporations whose incentives are opaque? The fear here is not sudden destruction but slow suffocation—the recognition that critical systems might be manipulated, withheld, or denied at decisive moments. Dependency, not detonation, becomes the foundation of coercion.

The asymmetry this creates is profound. A single nation or corporation with advanced AI capabilities can exert disproportionate influence over others without firing a shot. The capacity to surveil global communications, shape narratives through algorithmic recommendation systems, or disrupt supply chains through targeted cyber operations gives new meaning to the term "great power." Unlike nuclear weapons, which required vast state apparatuses and years of industrial effort, AI capabilities can emerge in smaller, more agile contexts. Yet their impact is amplified because they exploit the interconnectedness of global systems. One algorithm embedded in global logistics software can affect shipping lanes across continents; one breakthrough in natural language processing can tilt the balance of soft power in media and culture.

It is tempting to imagine AI as merely a set of tools—spreadsheets made faster, translations made smoother, predictions made sharper. But to see it in such narrow terms is to miss the wider transformation. AI functions as a force multiplier, bending the shape of entire systems rather than merely enhancing tasks within them. It can accelerate the pace of discovery in science, shift the efficiency of industries, or tilt electoral politics by manipulating flows of information. Like the atomic bomb, it introduces a discontinuity—a break so profound that it forces new strategies, doctrines, and survival mechanisms. The challenge is that this discontinuity unfolds not with a single event but through diffuse, ongoing integration.

The introduction of fire or gunpowder was visible, the mushroom cloud undeniable. AI's ascent is more difficult to pinpoint, which makes it more dangerous. The absence of spectacle lulls societies into complacency even as their dependencies deepen. The realisation often comes too late—that critical infrastructure is entangled, that sovereignty is compromised, that autonomy has been traded for efficiency. The algorithmic bomb detonates silently, not in cities reduced to rubble but in sovereignties quietly subordinated to systems they no longer control.

This chapter traces the logic of this transformation. It will show how AI stands in direct continuity with earlier leaps in human power, yet also why it is uniquely disruptive. It will explore how leverage is created invisibly—through markets, borders, and information flows—and why the stockpiles of the future are measured in data, compute, and talent rather than missiles or tanks. Finally, it will examine how fear itself has shifted: from the spectacle of annihilation to the silent manipulation of economies and societies. The purpose is not to paint AI as omnipotent, nor to reduce it to another technology among many, but to situate it accurately as the defining force multiplier of our time. To understand the algorithmic bomb is to understand not just a technological shift, but a profound reorganisation of power itself.

From Fire to Fission to Code

Power has never been distributed evenly, and throughout history, breakthroughs in technology have tilted the scales with such force that the very structure of civilisation was remade. Fire was the first such revolution. Its mastery gave humans more than warmth or cooked meals: it conferred control over environments, transformed diets, extended lifespans, and enabled the creation of communities around a shared resource. Fire was not merely a tool but a threshold—once crossed, it could not be uncrossed. Societies that learned to harness it thrived, while those without it were relegated to the margins of survival. In its embers lay the first lesson of technological asymmetry: control of a transformative power could elevate a group beyond the reach of others.

Gunpowder, centuries later, transformed the dynamics of conflict and empire. The fortified castle, once the ultimate symbol of security, was rendered obsolete as cannons reduced its walls to rubble. Those who mastered the chemistry of explosive power extended their reach across continents, toppling empires and redrawing borders. The Portuguese, armed with gunpowder weapons, secured naval supremacy in the fifteenth and sixteenth centuries, while states that lacked access to these new arsenals faced rapid decline. Gunpowder did not merely enhance warfare—it rewrote the logic of statehood and empire. It proved that technological breakthroughs could compress centuries of balance into moments of collapse, granting disproportionate power to the innovators.

The twentieth century's atomic bomb was the culmination of this trajectory. Unlike fire or gunpowder, nuclear fission did not merely shift the mechanics of war; it introduced existential stakes for the entire planet. One bomb could annihilate a city; a full exchange could erase human civilisation. The possession of nuclear weapons became the ultimate currency of geopolitical status, dividing the world into nuclear powers and those perpetually vulnerable to them. Yet the bomb's significance lay not only in its destructive capacity but in the doctrine it created: deterrence. Nations could no longer engage in direct conflict without risking mutual obliteration. Thus, nuclear weapons remade international politics as much as they altered warfare. They forced a new order premised on fear and restraint, demonstrating that technologies can reorganise power not simply through their use but through their potential.

Artificial intelligence now emerges as the next decisive leap in this lineage, but its nature makes it both more elusive and more pervasive. Unlike fire, gunpowder, or fission, AI does not present itself as a dramatic spectacle. There is no obvious moment of ignition, no battlefield revolution, no mushroom cloud. Instead, its power is exercised through integration—quietly embedded in financial systems, supply chains, medical research, military hardware, and political communication. This invisibility does not make it less consequential; rather, it makes it more insidious. AI is not a singular tool but a *force multiplier* that amplifies capabilities across every domain of human activity. It shapes entire systems of dominance rather than discrete confrontations.

The asymmetry it creates is subtler but no less decisive. In finance, the 2010 Flash Crash revealed how algorithms could destabilise global markets within minutes, triggering consequences that no human could foresee or control at comparable speed. Such events demonstrate that economic security—the foundation of national prosperity—can be disrupted not through bombs or sanctions but through code interacting at machine speed. In security, predictive policing systems already determine who is stopped or monitored, transferring decisions about justice from human officers to statistical models. Militarily, drones and autonomous systems rely on AI-driven targeting, compressing decision cycles from minutes to seconds and reducing human oversight. Across these domains, the same pattern emerges: the decisive power does not lie in destruction but in control, prediction, and manipulation.

To treat AI as merely a "tool" is to misunderstand its systemic nature. A hammer or rifle magnifies human capacity, but their scope is confined to the hands that wield them. AI, by contrast, scales autonomously once deployed. A single model can influence millions simultaneously, whether by filtering search results, shaping political discourse, or coordinating military operations. Its reach is exponential, not linear. Moreover, its influence compounds: the more data it processes, the better it becomes; the more widely it is adopted, the more indispensable it appears. *This compounding dynamic makes AI unlike any previous technology, for its power grows not only with use but with dependence.*

What is particularly striking is how AI redefines stockpiling. The twentieth century measured power in arsenals of missiles and warheads; the twenty-first century measures it in data reserves, compute capacity, and concentrations of talent. Each of these elements accumulates in ways that reinforce one another. Data feeds better models, which require greater compute, which in turn attract the world's most capable engineers and scientists. A nation or corporation that dominates in one dimension often finds itself accelerating across the others. This creates a feedback loop of advantage: the strong become stronger, and those without access to such resources are trapped in dependency.

Unlike nuclear stockpiles, which could be monitored through treaties and satellites, AI's arsenals are opaque and dispersed. Server farms, semiconductor fabs, and research labs do not broadcast their destructive capacity as clearly as missile silos. Yet they confer strategic leverage no less decisive. The ability to deny another nation access to advanced chips, or to monopolise cloud infrastructure, can shift geopolitical alignments without a single shot fired. The asymmetry is real but difficult to measure, making it all the more destabilising.

This raises the question of fear. During the Cold War, fear was visceral: the image of mushroom clouds and annihilation haunted every calculation. With AI, fear is diffuse. It is the fear of dependency—of finding one's critical infrastructure reliant on algorithms or compute controlled abroad. It is the fear of manipulation—of societies destabilised not by bombs but by information warfare conducted through algorithmic amplification of lies and divisions. It is the fear of exclusion—of being permanently locked out of technological advances that determine economic competitiveness. Unlike nuclear fear, which was immediate and spectacular, algorithmic fear is incremental and suffocating. It is not the terror of sudden death but the anxiety of gradual subordination.

Some argue that AI lacks the decisive, world-ending capacity of nuclear weapons and thus should not be considered in the same lineage. Yet this critique misses the structural reality. AI may not erase cities in an instant, but it can erode sovereignty, legitimacy, and stability in ways that are no less world-defining. If nuclear weapons froze the world into a precarious balance of deterrence, AI threatens to dissolve balance altogether, producing a hierarchy where the few who command its resources can dictate terms to the many who cannot. *The defining asymmetry of our century may not be between life and death, but between autonomy and dependence.*

What makes this moment so urgent is that the diffusion of AI is not even. While fire spread universally and gunpowder eventually proliferated, and even nuclear technologies could be copied at extraordinary cost, AI concentrates advantage at planetary scale in ways that resist easy replication. The infrastructure required to train cutting-edge models—the chips, electricity, data centres, and human expertise—is accessible to only a handful of nations and corporations. This concentration ensures that power will be exercised through bottlenecks, choke points, and dependencies, not through universal diffusion.

Seen in this light, AI is the successor to fire, gunpowder, and fission not because it resembles them but because it exceeds them. Each prior breakthrough reshaped the terms of survival and power. AI reshapes the conditions of agency itself: who decides, who predicts, who controls. It is not an accessory to existing structures but a new architecture, weaving itself into every dimension of sovereignty and governance. To ignore its systemic nature is to misunderstand the scale of the shift underway. To grasp it is to recognise that we stand at another threshold moment in the history of power—one where dominance is coded, not detonated, and where the decisive question is not who has the biggest arsenal of weapons, but who commands the architectures of intelligence.

Power Without Detonation

Power has traditionally been associated with force that leaves a visible mark—armies crossing borders, bombs levelling cities, currencies collapsing under sanctions. Yet in the twenty-first century, some of the most decisive expressions of power occur without spectacle. They leave no ruins, no smouldering landscapes, no monuments to destruction. Instead, they manifest as subtle disruptions to markets, shifts in public perception, or invisible changes in the movement of people and goods. Artificial intelligence sits at the centre of this transformation. It creates leverage not by detonating in moments of shock but by insinuating itself into the systems that underpin societies, shaping outcomes without announcing its presence. The ability to control without destruction, to dominate without conquest, represents one of the most consequential shifts in the history of power.

The 2010 Flash Crash stands as a pivotal example of this new dynamic. On a May afternoon, the Dow Jones Industrial Average plunged nearly a thousand points in minutes, wiping out almost a trillion dollars in market value before swiftly rebounding. No terrorist attack, no policy announcement, no human trader caused this. Instead, high-frequency trading algorithms interacted in ways no regulator had anticipated. Trades cascaded at machine speed, exploiting microsecond advantages invisible to human participants. The event revealed how fragile the world's financial architecture had become when governed by autonomous code. Though no lasting destruction occurred, the temporary evaporation of a trillion dollars underscored a profound truth: *markets can now be destabilised as dramatically by algorithms as they once were by artillery or embargo.* What appeared to be a glitch was, in reality, a demonstration of power without detonation—proof that leverage could be exerted by code alone.

This invisible leverage is not confined to economics. Consider the use of predictive policing algorithms. Ostensibly designed to allocate police resources efficiently, these systems generate "risk scores" that direct officers to patrol certain neighbourhoods, monitor specific groups, or identify individuals as potential future offenders. Yet the models are trained on historical data rife with biases, meaning they often amplify existing inequities. The critical point is not only about fairness, though that matters greatly; it is about authority. When decisions about who is stopped, questioned, or surveilled are determined by code, sovereignty itself is exercised invisibly. Citizens may believe they are subject to impartial systems, yet their daily experience of law and order is being structured by statistical patterns that no ordinary person can contest or even perceive. The state wields authority through algorithms, but the mechanisms are hidden from democratic oversight. Power is asserted not with riot police or martial law but through an opaque logic embedded in software.

On the battlefield, the implications are even starker. Modern drone warfare exemplifies how AI enables force projection without traditional confrontation. Autonomous or semi-autonomous targeting systems can identify potential threats faster than human operators, reducing the "kill chain" from minutes to seconds. The drones themselves can remain airborne for long periods, loitering over regions and providing constant surveillance, their presence shaping behaviour on the ground. Unlike the deployment of conventional troops, which signals clear intent and risk, AI-driven drones alter the strategic calculus. Their strikes may be precise, but the broader effect is psychological: populations live under constant watch, militaries extend reach without incurring domestic casualties, and governments wield lethal force without parliamentary debate or public visibility. The violence remains real, yet its orchestration is increasingly hidden in layers of code. Detonation is replaced by decision at a distance, structured by algorithms.

The defining feature of this new power is its invisibility. Fire left ash, gunpowder left smoke, and nuclear fission left wastelands. AI leaves none of these traces. Its impact is measured in altered probabilities, reweighted options, redirected flows. A border algorithm flags some travellers for secondary screening while letting others pass unexamined, reshaping mobility without the visible drama of walls or checkpoints. A content recommendation engine amplifies some voices and suppresses others, tilting political discourse without the overt censorship of book burnings or press bans. In each case, the exercise of power is real, but its mechanisms are hidden, diffused, and easily mistaken for neutral efficiency. This is why AI's leverage can be so profound: it colonises the background of social life, rendering its interventions invisible until their consequences have already accumulated.

Some optimists argue that this is an improvement—that power exercised without destruction represents a gentler world order. Yet such reasoning misses the critical reality that invisibility does not equate to benignity. When power operates without spectacle, it also operates without accountability. Nuclear testing provoked public outcry because the mushroom clouds could be seen; drone strikes often escape scrutiny because they occur far away and are reported only in aggregate. Financial crises caused by mismanaged algorithms are harder to politicise than wars, yet their effects on livelihoods can be just as devastating. *The absence of ruins does not mean the absence of victims.*

There is also a philosophical dimension to this shift. The philosopher Michel Foucault described modern power as operating less through sovereign command and more through diffuse systems of surveillance and discipline. AI represents the extension of this dynamic to its logical extreme. It allows power to operate continuously, subtly, and pervasively, shaping conduct not by direct force but by structuring the conditions under which decisions are made. A recommendation system does not tell you what to think, but by curating what you see, it shapes the horizon of what you can imagine. A predictive policing algorithm does not arrest anyone directly, but by guiding police presence, it influences who will be arrested. In both cases, the exercise of power is systemic rather than episodic. *This is power without detonation—not a blast, but a recalibration of the field itself.*

To grasp its significance, we must compare it with earlier models of coercion. During the Cold War, deterrence depended on the threat of catastrophic retaliation. The visible possibility of annihilation structured political order. With AI, the logic is reversed: it is not the visible threat but the invisible dependency that matters. States may not fear annihilation by algorithm, but they increasingly fear manipulation—of their markets, infrastructures, or citizens' perceptions. Dependency on foreign AI systems creates vulnerabilities that can be exploited without any act resembling traditional warfare. A trading algorithm subtly favouring one nation's firms, a navigation system that subtly delays shipments, a social media algorithm amplifying discontent—all are forms of coercion whose effectiveness lies precisely in their subtlety.

The tension here lies in perception. Spectacular violence galvanises resistance; invisible power engenders resignation. Citizens may rally against foreign invasions, but how does one rally against an algorithm one cannot see? States may protest territorial incursions, but how do they protest biased predictive models designed abroad? The challenge of accountability is compounded by the fact that many of these systems are created and maintained not by states but by corporations. The frontier of power is not merely geopolitical but techno-commercial, exercised by entities that operate across borders yet owe allegiance to none.

This is why AI as power without detonation is more than a technological shift; it is a reorganisation of sovereignty itself. It blurs the distinction between domestic and foreign, civilian and military, public and private. It shifts the locus of authority from institutions we can see to algorithms we cannot interrogate. And it creates a form of leverage that is difficult to contest precisely because it does not manifest as force. The absence of smoke and fire is not a sign of weakness; it is the mark of a new kind of dominance.

Understanding this shift is not merely an intellectual exercise. It is essential for anyone who wishes to grasp the geopolitics of the present century. To overlook the power of algorithms because they do not detonate is to miss the way the world is being reshaped—quietly, invisibly, but decisively.

The Invisible Arsenal

For most of modern history, a nation's strength could be measured by the visibility of its stockpiles. Steel mills, shipyards, oil reserves, and missile silos stood as tangible symbols of power, markers of industrial and military might that allies and adversaries alike could count and fear. Today, the calculus has shifted. The most valuable arsenals are not made of tanks or shells, but of resources that cannot be weighed or paraded. They are built from data, compute, and human talent. Unlike missiles that corrode with time or oil that burns and disappears, these new stockpiles accumulate in ways that are self-reinforcing. *Algorithmic power compounds: the more a nation possesses, the faster it can generate more, and the harder it becomes for rivals to catch up.*

The analogy to weapons stockpiles is deliberate, for these resources serve the same purpose: they confer leverage, deterrence, and advantage in contests of power. Yet the nature of these arsenals is different. A nuclear warhead sits inert until it is deployed, but data can be mined continuously; compute capacity works day and night; talent produces breakthroughs that open entirely new domains of competition. The twentieth century's arms races were about accumulation followed by standoff. The twenty-first century's algorithmic competition is about acceleration—how fast a nation or corporation can expand its reserves relative to others. *It is not simply about what you have, but about the flywheel of advantage your resources create.*

Consider data. The comparison to oil is apt in the sense that both are raw materials with extraordinary economic and strategic value. But data is more insidious because its extraction rarely announces itself. Social media platforms collect behavioural traces from billions of people; sensors in cities record movements, purchases, and preferences; military surveillance gathers terabytes of video, signals, and biometrics. Unlike oil, which is finite and contested at the source, data reproduces endlessly, and its value increases when aggregated at scale. The more data you hold, the more sophisticated your models become, which in turn allows you to generate still more data through new products, new efficiencies, and deeper surveillance. China's advantage here is not only its population size but its political capacity to integrate personal, commercial, and state data streams. The United States and its tech corporations, meanwhile, enjoy dominance through global platforms that harvest information across borders. Smaller nations, lacking either massive populations or platforms with planetary reach, are left as data suppliers rather than sovereign owners.

Compute represents the second pillar of the invisible arsenal. In the Cold War, nuclear capabilities depended on uranium enrichment and missile delivery systems—complex, expensive, and centralised. Today's equivalent is the semiconductor supply chain. Advanced chips enable the training of large AI models, and the countries capable of producing or securing them control the pace of algorithmic advancement. Taiwan's Taiwan Semiconductor Manufacturing Company (TSMC) has become one of the most critical nodes in global power, its fabrication facilities producing chips essential not only to consumer electronics but to military-grade AI systems. Export controls by the United States on advanced semiconductors to China are therefore not mere trade policy; they are acts of strategic containment, designed to slow the accumulation of algorithmic capacity by a rival power. Compute is not fungible in the way oil or grain is—it requires intricate infrastructures of production, immense energy inputs, and highly skilled engineers. As such, it creates choke points and dependencies, giving outsized influence to the few nations and firms that control its production.

Talent, the third pillar, is perhaps the most overlooked yet decisive. Algorithms may be executed by machines, but their design and refinement depend on human ingenuity. The clustering of talent in places like Silicon Valley, Beijing, Toronto, or London creates intellectual ecosystems where breakthroughs emerge not in isolation but through dense networks of collaboration and competition. Unlike natural resources, which can be discovered anywhere, talent is cultivated through education, funding, and opportunity. Once established, these clusters become self-reinforcing. Talented individuals migrate to where others of their calibre already work, attracted by cutting-edge research and lucrative compensation. Nations that succeed in cultivating and retaining AI talent gain a compounding advantage, while those that cannot often see their brightest minds absorbed into foreign labs or corporations, further widening the gap. Talent mobility thus becomes a battleground for algorithmic sovereignty, as visas, scholarships, and corporate acquisitions serve as instruments of competition.

What makes these arsenals distinctive is their compounding nature. In nuclear arms races, the marginal value of each additional warhead eventually diminished once mutually assured destruction was guaranteed. The stockpiling of AI resources, however, produces increasing returns.

More data improves models; better models generate more user engagement or intelligence value, which in turn produces more data. Greater compute enables more complex architectures, which attract more talent, which produces further innovations. Unlike the static deterrence of nuclear weapons, algorithmic power accelerates, creating widening asymmetries over time. The gap between leaders and laggards does not stabilise—it grows.

This compounding dynamic challenges conventional thinking about arms control and balance of power. Nuclear parity was possible because the destructive potential of the weapons reached a ceiling: once both sides could annihilate each other, accumulation became redundant. With AI, no such ceiling exists. There is no saturation point at which more data, more compute, or more talent ceases to matter. The frontiers of application—from biotechnology to cyber warfare to governance—remain open, ensuring that every increment of additional capacity can translate into new domains of influence. This creates a strategic environment not of equilibrium but of perpetual competition, where falling behind risks permanent subordination.

Critics might argue that AI systems are widely accessible, that open-source models and consumer-grade hardware democratise the technology. While it is true that basic AI tools are more broadly available than nuclear weapons ever were, this misses the distinction between accessibility and strategic dominance. Open-source models may diffuse knowledge, but cutting-edge performance remains tied to those with the largest datasets, the most powerful compute clusters, and the deepest pools of expertise. A small state or start-up can build useful systems, but it cannot compete at the same level as a superpower or trillion-dollar corporation investing billions annually in AI research. The gap is not closed by openness; it is widened by scale.

The invisible arsenal also complicates the role of corporations in geopolitics. Unlike nuclear warheads, which were tightly controlled by states, today's algorithmic resources are often concentrated in private firms. Microsoft, Google, Amazon, Alibaba, and Tencent manage vast data flows and compute infrastructures that rival or exceed those of many governments. Their capacity to hire, retain, and direct top talent places them at the frontier of innovation. States, rather than monopolising the invisible arsenal, increasingly find themselves dependent on corporate actors who may not align with national interests. This blurring of public and private complicates traditional notions of sovereignty, as the resources decisive for national power lie partly in the hands of shareholder-driven entities. The arsenal is no longer housed in military bunkers but in corporate data centres.

The compounding nature of algorithmic arsenals also creates a feedback loop in global inequality. Nations or firms that fall behind in one domain—lacking compute infrastructure, for instance—soon find themselves disadvantaged in attracting talent, which in turn limits their ability to generate data-rich platforms. Each gap reinforces the others, leaving some countries locked into dependency. Conversely, those with an initial lead consolidate their dominance across multiple domains. This is why the race for algorithmic power feels more unforgiving than previous technological competitions. In earlier industrial revolutions, latecomers could catch up by adopting established techniques. In the algorithmic race, the window for catching up narrows rapidly as leaders entrench their advantages.

There is an ethical dimension to recognising data, compute, and talent as arsenals. Stockpiling nuclear weapons carried an inherent acknowledgement of their destructive purpose. Stockpiling AI resources is often framed as innovation, growth, or security. Yet the underlying dynamic is the same: an arms race in which accumulation creates leverage, fear, and dependency. The difference is that the weapons are invisible, their impacts diffused across societies rather than concentrated in spectacular moments of detonation. This invisibility makes public scrutiny weaker, yet the stakes are just as high. The capacity to dominate through algorithms may not leave craters in landscapes, but it can erode sovereignty, reshape economies, and reconfigure the balance of global order.

To understand the invisible arsenal is to recognise that the strategic resources of our time are not physical stockpiles but compounding capacities. Data, compute, and talent form the triad that defines algorithmic power, and the nations or corporations that command them are constructing a new hierarchy of dominance. Unlike past arsenals, these cannot be easily counted or inspected. They are dispersed, cumulative, and often hidden behind the innocuous language of platforms and services. Yet they confer real power—the power to predict, to manipulate, to innovate, and ultimately to govern. This is the arsenal of the algorithmic age, and its invisibility does not diminish its force; it magnifies it.

The New Fear Factor

Fear has always been the foundation of deterrence. In the twentieth century, fear was embodied in a single, unforgettable image: the mushroom cloud.

Nuclear weapons created an existential dread so absolute that it reordered global politics around the prospect of mutual annihilation. Deterrence worked not because nuclear war was waged but because the fear of it paralysed adversaries. The world lived under the shadow of catastrophe, knowing that one miscalculation could erase entire cities. Today, that same visceral fear is less visible, but it has not disappeared. It has migrated from the spectacle of annihilation to the subtle anxiety of dependency. Instead of mushroom clouds, societies now fear the silent manipulation of their economies, infrastructures, and collective consciousness by algorithms they do not control.

This new fear is harder to dramatise but no less consequential. Nuclear deterrence was anchored in clarity: weapons were countable, the logic of mutually assured destruction was grimly rational, and the enemy was visible. With artificial intelligence, the lines are murkier. Power is not measured in warheads but in datasets, chips, and the talent to turn them into systems of prediction and control. The threat is not instant destruction but incremental subordination. What nations dread is not an adversary's bomb but their own reliance on algorithms and infrastructures designed elsewhere. Fear is no longer the anticipation of annihilation; it is the gnawing recognition of dependence.

Consider global financial systems. When the Flash Crash of 2010 erased nearly a trillion dollars of value in under an hour, the fear it revealed was not of a hostile strike but of vulnerability to invisible systems. Markets that underpin national prosperity can now be destabilised not by armies but by lines of code. The fear factor here is insidious: governments know that their economic stability could be compromised by algorithms operating outside their jurisdiction, controlled by actors they cannot easily identify or hold accountable. Unlike nuclear standoffs, which had thresholds and doctrines, algorithmic disruptions occur without warning, often without clear attribution. Fear arises not from imminent catastrophe but from the awareness that the foundations of prosperity are beyond sovereign control.

Border security offers another perspective. Whereas the Cold War was defined by tanks, walls, and missile shields, contemporary borders are increasingly governed by predictive algorithms and biometric systems. States adopt these technologies in pursuit of efficiency and safety, yet dependency follows swiftly. A government reliant on foreign AI systems for border management lives with the constant fear that these systems could fail, be manipulated, or be withdrawn. This is not fear of invasion in the conventional sense but of paralysis: the inability to manage sovereign functions without permission or support from external providers. Such dependence undermines the very concept of autonomy, producing a form of deterrence where adversaries need not threaten destruction—they need only hint at disruption.

The battlefield provides a still sharper view of the new fear factor. Nuclear deterrence relied on the threat of massive retaliation; AI-driven warfare relies on the threat of selective paralysis. A swarm of drones guided by adversarial algorithms does not need to level cities to produce terror; it need only demonstrate that an opponent's traditional defences are obsolete. States now fear not just the use of AI weapons but the inability to counter them. The terror lies not in the scale of destruction but in the exposure of weakness, the recognition that one's own arsenals can be rendered irrelevant by superior algorithms. This fear is compounded by the opacity of AI: militaries may not even understand why their systems fail, only that they do.

The psychological landscape of deterrence is thus being rewritten. Nuclear fear was collective and immediate—images of devastation mobilised publics and shaped grand strategy. Algorithmic fear is diffuse and enduring, affecting daily governance, economic planning, and social cohesion. Citizens live in an environment where information itself can be manipulated at scale. Disinformation campaigns powered by AI-generated content can erode trust in institutions without firing a shot. The fear this generates is not the terror of sudden death but the anxiety of not knowing what is real. If nuclear deterrence thrived on the visibility of destruction, algorithmic deterrence thrives on the invisibility of manipulation. *The most frightening attacks are the ones societies may not even realise are happening until the damage is irreversible.*

What makes this fear structurally powerful is its asymmetry. Nuclear deterrence created a balance of terror; both sides could destroy each other, creating a form of equilibrium. Algorithmic dependence creates hierarchy, not parity. A nation reliant on another's algorithms, compute infrastructure, or data pipelines cannot deter in kind. It is locked into a subordinate relationship, compelled to comply not by the threat of annihilation but by the risk of exclusion. Fear shifts from the calculus of destruction to the calculus of access: the fear of being cut off from systems that sustain the economy, manage borders, or even govern social interaction. Dependency becomes a weapon as potent as any arsenal, because it creates deterrence without reciprocity.

There are those who argue that fear of AI manipulation lacks the visceral clarity that made nuclear deterrence stable. Citizens may accept algorithmic governance in exchange for convenience, or governments may underestimate the risks until crises occur. Yet this underestimation is itself part of the new fear factor. The opacity of algorithms ensures that vulnerabilities remain hidden until they are exploited. A society may only realise the extent of its dependence when a system fails catastrophically—a cyberattack shutting down critical infrastructure, a supply chain paralysed by AI-driven logistics disruptions, or a national election swayed by algorithmic disinformation. The fear here is retrospective: the recognition that dependency was deeper and more dangerous than anyone admitted.

What distinguishes this new form of deterrence is that it is continuous rather than episodic. Nuclear weapons were brandished in moments of crisis; AI systems are integrated into everyday governance. The fear they create is therefore lived daily, not only at moments of geopolitical brinkmanship. A nation may not think about nuclear war every time it launches a satellite, but it must think about algorithmic dependence every time it manages financial transactions, secures its borders, or maintains public trust in information flows. This constant awareness creates a more pervasive form of vulnerability. *Fear becomes ambient, a condition of existence rather than a threat of extraordinary moments.*

At its core, the shift from nuclear deterrence to algorithmic dependence represents a transformation in how power disciplines societies. The mushroom cloud demanded attention; algorithmic manipulation escapes it. Nuclear arsenals were finite and could be monitored; algorithmic arsenals are compounding and hidden. Deterrence once relied on spectacle; it now relies on subtle coercion through dependency. The fear factor has not diminished—it has become more intimate, woven into the infrastructures on which daily life depends. To live in the algorithmic age is to live not under the shadow of annihilation but under the constant pressure of silent leverage.

Chapter 2

Data Colonies and Digital Empires

Every empire has been built on control of a resource that others could not do without. For Rome, it was grain; for Britain, coal and naval trade routes; for twentieth-century powers, oil. Each resource reshaped geopolitics, created dependencies, and determined who held structural advantage. Today, the most valuable resource is no longer material but informational: data. It has become the raw material of the future, the lifeblood of artificial intelligence, and the currency through which influence is increasingly exercised. What makes data distinctive is not just its value but its distribution and extraction. It is produced everywhere yet concentrated in the hands of those who know how to harvest and exploit it. Like oil in the twentieth century, it is politically charged, unevenly accessible, and transformative in its applications. But unlike oil, which lies under the ground, data resides in the flows of human life—our communications, movements, habits, and decisions. Whoever controls these flows commands leverage over societies, markets, and states.

The structural advantage is already evident. Nations with large populations generate vast datasets simply by scale, while those with extensive surveillance infrastructures can capture more granular detail about their citizens. China exemplifies this dual advantage. Its population of over a billion ensures a steady stream of behavioural data, and its political system permits a level of surveillance integration that other societies would resist. The United States, by contrast, has leveraged global digital platforms—social media, search engines, and e-commerce—to harvest data not only from its own citizens but from billions worldwide. Smaller nations, even technologically advanced ones, cannot match the volume or reach of these giants. This imbalance creates a hierarchy in which data-rich states have a structural edge in developing and deploying AI, while data-poor states risk permanent subordination. *The map of global power is being redrawn not by borders but by the density of data flows a nation can command.*

Yet the analogy with oil obscures as much as it reveals. Unlike oil, data does not require drilling rigs or shipping lanes. Its extraction is largely invisible, often occurring without the knowledge or consent of those who generate it. Corporations track user behaviour through apps, browsers, and devices, amassing detailed profiles that are then monetised or fed into machine learning systems. Governments engage in their own forms of surveillance, ranging from targeted counter-terrorism monitoring to mass collection of communications metadata. This extraction is borderless. A European teenager's browsing habits can be collected by an American company, stored in a server farm in Asia, analysed by engineers in California, and ultimately used to optimise advertising campaigns in Africa. Unlike natural resources, which could be seized only through physical conquest, data is extracted silently across frontiers, often under the guise of services freely given. This mirrors the asymmetries of colonialism: resources flow outwards from peripheries to centres of power, enriching the latter while leaving the former dependent and exposed.

Dependency is not a side effect of this system; it is its defining logic. Smaller nations increasingly rely on AI systems developed and owned by foreign tech superpowers. A government may adopt American software to manage healthcare or education, or Chinese surveillance technologies to police its cities. On the surface, these systems promise efficiency and modernisation. In reality, they entrench reliance. The algorithms are trained on data the host nation does not own, the models are updated in labs abroad, and the compute infrastructures remain under foreign control. Over time, sovereignty is hollowed out. Decisions central to national governance are mediated by systems that cannot be independently audited or altered. *This is the dependency trap of the digital age: sovereignty outsourced not through colonisation of territory but through colonisation of infrastructure.*

The implications are profound. Just as colonial economies were structured to serve metropolitan interests, today's digital dependencies shape the political and economic futures of smaller states. A nation whose judicial system relies on predictive analytics from a foreign corporation is constrained in how it governs; a country whose financial systems depend on cloud infrastructure owned abroad is limited in how it regulates. Even military autonomy can be compromised: surveillance drones, cybersecurity platforms, or command systems often arrive packaged with dependencies that tie a state's security to foreign providers. Dependency is not only economic but existential, binding states to systems they cannot control but cannot afford to abandon.

Resistance, however, is emerging. India's data localisation laws seek to ensure that data generated by Indian citizens remains within national borders, an attempt to reclaim sovereignty over informational flows. The European Union's General Data Protection Regulation (GDPR) represents another early attempt at resistance, enforcing strict conditions on data collection and transfer. These measures represent a recognition that control over data is control over the future. Yet their limitations are equally revealing. Data localisation may ensure storage, but it does not guarantee capacity to process or exploit the data. GDPR may protect individual rights, but it does not dismantle the dominance of corporations whose platforms are global by design. Resistance exists, but it remains reactive, fragmented, and uneven.

The philosophical dimension of these struggles should not be overlooked. If sovereignty in the industrial age was defined by control over physical resources, sovereignty in the algorithmic age is defined by control over informational flows. Yet sovereignty is being diluted precisely because these flows do not respect borders. A citizen's data is simultaneously a personal asset, a commercial commodity, and a geopolitical resource. States struggle to regulate this ambiguity, corporations exploit it, and citizens are left uncertain about who ultimately governs their digital selves. The result is a new form of imperialism—one not marked by flags planted on foreign soil but by infrastructures of extraction that turn human life into raw material for distant powers.

This chapter traces these dynamics in depth. It situates data as the raw material of the future, explains how extraction without borders replicates colonial patterns, analyses the dependency trap that smaller nations fall into, and examines efforts at resistance and reclamation. The purpose is not to argue that data is simply "the new oil," but to show how its distinctive qualities—its invisibility, its borderlessness, its compounding value—make it the foundation of digital empires. To understand data as a resource is to recognise the profound asymmetries it generates, the dependencies it entrenches, and the possibilities, however limited, of reclaiming control. The age of data colonies has already begun, and the fate of digital sovereignty will determine the hierarchies of power for decades to come.

The Raw Material of the Future

Every age has been defined by a resource that shaped both prosperity and power. For much of the twentieth century, that resource was oil. Nations with abundant reserves commanded geopolitical attention, corporations that controlled drilling and refining became industrial giants, and military strategies revolved around securing supply lines and choke points. Oil was never just energy; it was leverage. The resource determined who could industrialise, who could project power, and who remained dependent on others. Today, the role once played by oil is being assumed by data. It is the critical input for artificial intelligence, the infrastructure of digital economies, and the basis on which decisions—economic, political, and military—are increasingly made. Like oil, it is unevenly distributed, politically contested, and indispensable. Unlike oil, however, its extraction is largely invisible and its value multiplies the more it is used. To understand data is to understand the foundations of twenty-first century power.

What makes data so potent is not simply its abundance but its compounding utility. Oil is consumed when burned; data grows in value through repeated use. A single dataset on consumer behaviour can be mined for purchasing patterns, repurposed to train recommendation engines, and sold to third parties for targeted advertising. When combined with other datasets, its predictive power increases exponentially. This characteristic makes data less a commodity than an endlessly recyclable asset. The more you have, the more valuable it becomes, and the more competitive your algorithms grow. *Data, in other words, feeds on itself, and its compounding nature locks advantage into the hands of those who control it.*

Yet, despite its ubiquity, data is not distributed equally. Nations with larger populations produce larger volumes of it, often without any additional effort. A billion people using mobile phones generate an enormous flow of location data, communications metadata, and behavioural traces, all of which can be captured and repurposed. Surveillance capacity further enhances this advantage. States that maintain extensive monitoring of their citizens can gather higher-quality data than those constrained by privacy norms or legal safeguards. China exemplifies this dual structural advantage. Its vast population provides a constant supply of behavioural data, while its centralised political system enables integration of financial records, facial recognition footage, and online activity into massive state-controlled databases. This creates a reservoir of training material for AI systems unmatched by most other countries. By contrast, smaller nations—even wealthy ones—struggle to generate enough data internally to compete at scale. Their sovereignty in the digital age is therefore precarious, dependent on external platforms that both supply services and extract information in return.

The corporate dimension deepens the imbalance. American technology giants such as Google, Amazon, and Meta operate global platforms that harvest data across borders, often with limited oversight by local governments. A user in Nairobi or Jakarta provides just as much value to a Silicon Valley data centre as a user in New York, yet the economic and strategic benefits accrue largely to the corporations and the state that regulates them. This borderless extraction mirrors colonial logics: resources flow outward from peripheries to centres of power, enriching the latter while leaving the former dependent on imported technologies. Where colonial empires once controlled railways, shipping lanes, and plantations, digital empires control cloud services, search engines, and social platforms. *Data is the new extractive frontier, and its colonisation is already well underway.*

The political charge surrounding data stems from its dual character: it is both personal and geopolitical. On one level, it represents the intimate details of individual lives—our movements, purchases, communications, and preferences. On another, it aggregates into a resource that powers national economies, drives military innovation, and enables geopolitical leverage. This duality complicates governance. Citizens demand privacy and autonomy, yet states recognise that sovereignty in the algorithmic age depends on capturing and controlling flows of data. The tension is acute. Europe has sought to balance these pressures through regulatory frameworks such as the General Data Protection Regulation (GDPR), emphasising individual rights. China has chosen the opposite path, prioritising state control over privacy in the name of collective power. The United States has largely allowed private corporations to dominate the landscape, with the state leveraging corporate datasets for its own strategic purposes. These divergent models illustrate that data governance is not merely a technical issue but a profound political choice.

The structural advantage conferred by data can already be seen in AI performance. Large language models, facial recognition systems, and predictive analytics all improve dramatically with greater volumes of high-quality data. This means that states and corporations with access to massive datasets accelerate further ahead, while those without fall behind. Unlike oil, which could be traded and stockpiled, data is rarely shared across rivals. It is hoarded, protected, and expanded relentlessly. This creates a feedback loop: the more data one controls, the more powerful one's AI systems become, which in turn attract more users, generating still more data. This cycle ensures that advantage compounds, leaving latecomers with diminishing chances to catch up.

To appreciate the geopolitical stakes, one need only look at the contest between the United States and China. Both recognise that data underpins not only economic competitiveness but also military capability and ideological influence. Surveillance data from smart cities informs domestic governance and counter-terrorism operations. Military sensor data trains autonomous systems for battlefield decision-making. Global data flows, captured through platforms and undersea cables, provide strategic intelligence. The struggle for technological leadership is therefore inseparable from the struggle to command data. Smaller nations are drawn into this competition not as equals but as suppliers of raw informational material, often ceding control to one bloc or another in exchange for access to AI-driven services.

Philosophically, the rise of data as a resource forces us to reconsider the meaning of sovereignty. In earlier centuries, sovereignty meant control of land and borders. In the twentieth century, it expanded to include control over energy and industrial capacity. Today, it extends to control over data. Yet unlike territory, data is not fixed in place; it is constantly flowing, reproduced every time a transaction is made or a message sent. This fluidity makes sovereignty harder to exercise. It is not enough to guard borders; states must now regulate platforms, manage infrastructures, and oversee algorithms that operate transnationally. The challenge is daunting because the architectures of data extraction were designed by corporations to transcend jurisdiction, not to respect it.

The analogy to oil remains instructive but limited. Oil was finite, its reserves identifiable, its trade governed by markets and treaties. Data is infinite in generation, impossible to fully track, and far more politicised in its governance. Oil fuelled industrial revolutions; data fuels cognitive and algorithmic revolutions. Oil could be hoarded; data grows in value when shared and aggregated. Oil consumption produced visible externalities like pollution; data exploitation produces subtler ones like bias, surveillance creep, and erosion of trust. These differences make data an even more complex resource to govern than oil ever was.

For nations, the lesson is stark. To be data-poor is to risk exclusion from the most transformative technological advances of the century. To be data-rich is to wield disproportionate leverage over others. Yet to be data-rich without the means to process and exploit that data—through compute infrastructure and talent—risks squandering the advantage. Control of data is necessary but not sufficient. It must be integrated into an ecosystem that can transform it into intelligence, prediction, and action. *The raw material of the future is not data alone, but the capacity to mobilise it effectively.*

The age of data has already reordered hierarchies of power. It privileges large populations and surveillance states, empowers corporations with global reach, and exposes smaller nations to new forms of dependency. To grasp data as the raw material of the future is to understand not just a technological trend but the structural foundations of a new geopolitics—one in which sovereignty is contested not on battlefields but in databases, platforms, and the invisible infrastructures of digital life.

Extraction Without Borders

The most valuable resource of the twenty-first century moves without ships, pipelines, or customs inspections. It flows silently through fibre-optic cables, across satellite links, and through the cloud infrastructures that knit the digital world together. This resource is data, and unlike oil or minerals, it can be harvested in one country, processed in another, and monetised in yet another, often without the knowledge—let alone the consent—of the people who generated it. Corporations and states have perfected the art of global extraction, drawing value from populations far beyond their jurisdictional reach. The practice is not accidental; it mirrors earlier colonial patterns of resource plunder, where wealth was siphoned from the periphery to the centre, leaving the sources of extraction dependent, exposed, and structurally weakened.

What makes data extraction distinctive is its invisibility. When European powers stripped colonies of spices, cotton, or gold, the absence was tangible. Today, data is lifted from phones, social networks, hospitals, and workplaces in ways most people scarcely perceive. The trade-offs are hidden in terms and conditions documents that no one reads, in consent forms written to obscure rather than clarify, and in the default settings of apps designed to collect as much as possible. This asymmetry of knowledge replicates the asymmetry of power. Populations in the Global South, for instance, contribute vast streams of behavioural and biometric data every day via smartphones and digital services, but the economic benefits flow primarily to servers in California, Virginia, or Shenzhen. *Extraction without borders is not just a metaphor: it is the operating logic of the digital economy.*

Consider the case of social media platforms. Facebook, now Meta, has more users in India, Indonesia, and the Philippines than in the United

States, yet the value created from these markets overwhelmingly accrues to the company's headquarters. Advertising revenue harvested from attention spans in Lagos or Manila strengthens balance sheets in Menlo Park. The model echoes the colonial plantation: labour and raw material come from distant territories, profit flows to the metropole. The platforms provide utility to users, but the deeper benefits—AI training data, behavioural insights, predictive analytics—are captured at the core.

The healthcare sector offers an equally revealing example. Genomic databases and medical imaging datasets are central to advances in personalised medicine and AI-driven diagnostics. Yet much of the genomic data used by Western pharmaceutical companies has been sourced from populations in Africa, South Asia, and Latin America, often under vague promises of contributing to "scientific progress." Once collected, the data is exported to research labs and commercialised in ways that rarely return benefits to the communities of origin. The ethical questions here are profound: should the health data of poorer populations serve as the raw material for pharmaceutical profits in richer ones, especially when those same populations cannot afford the drugs developed? The pattern is hauntingly familiar to scholars of resource politics: the periphery supplies, the core capitalises.

Corporate extraction operates alongside and often in collaboration with state extraction. Governments today view access to data not just as an economic resource but as a matter of national security. The United States compels data sharing through surveillance alliances such as Five Eyes. China, meanwhile, requires companies within its jurisdiction to provide access to user data under the banner of national security and social stability. Russia, India, and others have pursued data localisation laws in an attempt to prevent uncontrolled outward flows. But even localisation does not fully prevent extraction. Cloud computing contracts, app ownership, and infrastructure dependencies all provide pathways through which data crosses borders, often invisibly.

For many smaller nations, participation in the digital economy effectively means surrendering sovereignty over informational resources. Cloud storage services operated by Amazon, Microsoft, or Alibaba host the bulk of state and corporate data in countries that lack their own infrastructure. This creates a dependency not unlike that of colonial economies reliant on foreign-owned railroads and ports. When an African government stores public health data on US-owned servers, or when a Southeast Asian bank relies on Chinese fintech platforms, the critical infrastructure of sovereignty is externalised. The dependency is not only technological but political, leaving states vulnerable to the strategic priorities of the host powers. *Digital sovereignty has become inseparable from questions of data extraction.*

Some might argue that unlike colonial commodities, data extraction does not impoverish the source. After all, a dataset is not diminished when copied. Yet this perspective misses the structural asymmetry. The raw information may remain, but the capacity to process, analyse, and monetise it is concentrated elsewhere. Just as resource-rich colonies were often left dependent on foreign companies for processing and export, data-rich nations may find themselves dependent on foreign corporations for computational capacity and algorithmic expertise. The surplus value lies not in possession but in transformation. Without compute power, skilled labour, and global distribution channels, raw data is inert.

The analogy with colonialism extends further when one considers the dynamics of consent and coercion. Colonial extraction often proceeded under the guise of contracts, treaties, or nominal compensation—arrangements heavily tilted in favour of the coloniser. Similarly, today's digital extraction often proceeds under the cover of "user consent." When citizens of developing countries sign up for social media or mobile payment systems, they technically "agree" to data collection. But in practice, this consent is neither informed nor voluntary: alternatives are scarce, and the documents are deliberately opaque. The result is a global asymmetry of informational power justified by the rhetoric of choice.

At the geopolitical level, data extraction without borders has become a strategic contest. Control over global platforms is a form of power projection. When TikTok spreads across Western markets, it exports not only entertainment but also behavioural telemetry that feeds back into Chinese-owned systems. When Google dominates search in Africa, it shapes not only information access but also the future of AI trained on linguistic data from those regions. States understand this dynamic well. This is why the US government has sought to restrict Huawei's role in 5G networks, why India banned dozens of Chinese apps after border tensions, and why Europe has tightened restrictions on US tech giants. The underlying issue is not just security or privacy but sovereignty over flows of informational wealth.

The philosophical implications are striking. Borders, once the fundamental markers of sovereignty, have little meaning when the most valuable resource can flow out of a country through the click of an app update. International law was built to regulate the movement of goods, capital, and people, but it remains ill-equipped to regulate flows of data. Attempts at regulation, such as the EU's GDPR, represent one model: constraining extraction by strengthening individual rights. China represents another: strengthening state control at the expense of individual privacy. Both approaches highlight the same reality—that data extraction without borders is unsustainable if left entirely to the market.

Yet resistance remains uneven. Wealthy states with regulatory capacity can push back against unrestricted extraction, as seen with the EU's antitrust cases against US tech firms. Middle powers such as India seek to leverage their vast populations to demand localisation and data-sharing concessions. But smaller nations often lack the bargaining power or technical capacity to do the same. They become informational peripheries, harvested for value while struggling to assert sovereignty. The effect is to entrench a new global hierarchy: digital empires at the core, data colonies at the margins.

The challenge, then, is not simply to recognise the parallels with historical extraction but to understand their implications for global order. Just as the scramble for resources in earlier centuries reshaped geopolitics, the scramble for data is redrawing maps of dependence and influence. Corporations operate like quasi-states, with infrastructures and populations that rival those of nations. States, in turn, adopt corporate tactics, embedding extraction into their global strategies. The distinction between public and private power blurs. What remains clear is that extraction without borders is neither neutral nor benign. It redistributes wealth, reconfigures sovereignty, and creates new forms of inequality that will define the geopolitics of the coming decades.

The Dependency Trap

Sovereignty in the digital age no longer hinges solely on control over borders, armies, or currencies. It now depends on who commands the algorithms that run economies, mediate communication, and increasingly govern political decision-making. Smaller nations, in particular, face a growing dilemma: their economic development, social governance, and security infrastructures are becoming dependent on AI systems designed, owned, and maintained by a handful of tech superpowers. The phenomenon echoes older forms of dependency, where peripheral economies relied on industrial powers for machinery or finance, but its stakes are sharper and its consequences more encompassing. *To be excluded from advanced AI ecosystems today is to risk stagnation; to be fully included is to accept a loss of control.*

Dependency often begins innocuously, through the adoption of digital platforms marketed as tools of empowerment. Cloud services promise efficiency, predictive policing tools promise safety, and AI-driven agriculture promises higher yields. For countries with limited domestic research capacity, such offerings appear irresistible. Yet embedded in the code are structural dependencies. The datasets, training algorithms, and updates remain controlled by foreign corporations. This leaves client states perpetually reliant on the goodwill, commercial priorities, and geopolitical alignments of the providers. The trap is subtle: the very tools that enable participation in the digital economy ensure long-term subordination within it.

Healthcare provides a telling illustration. Many low- and middle-income countries have turned to AI diagnostics to compensate for shortages of medical professionals. These systems, trained on datasets from hospitals in North America or Europe, are supplied by multinational firms. While they can improve health outcomes, they also lock hospitals and governments into ongoing licensing fees, data-sharing obligations, and dependence on proprietary updates. The sovereignty cost becomes clear when governments cannot meaningfully audit or alter the models. What appears to be capacity-building in the short term risks being dependency-building in the long term. *Health systems built on borrowed intelligence remain structurally beholden to their originators.*

The financial sector demonstrates the dependency trap at a national scale. AI-driven credit scoring and mobile payment systems have spread rapidly across the developing world, often leapfrogging traditional banking. Yet the algorithms that determine who qualifies for credit, at what rates, and under what conditions are controlled by a small cluster of global fintech firms. In Kenya, M-Pesa revolutionised payments, but its expansion also revealed how entire economies could become reliant on infrastructures owned by corporations beyond democratic oversight. Dependency here is not just economic but epistemic: when creditworthiness is defined by opaque AI systems, local regulators lose the ability to set standards of fairness within their own jurisdictions.

The geopolitical stakes are starkest in the domain of security. Predictive policing, border control systems, and surveillance infrastructures are increasingly AI-driven. Governments with limited domestic capacity often import these systems wholesale from China, the United States, or Israel. In doing so, they cede not only control over sensitive data but also strategic autonomy. A Latin American country relying on Chinese facial recognition technology, for example, finds its security sector intertwined with Beijing's commercial and strategic interests. Should political tensions rise, that infrastructure could be leveraged as a bargaining chip. *Dependency in the AI era is not passive reliance but active vulnerability.*

It is tempting to suggest that smaller nations could simply develop their own systems to avoid dependency. In practice, this is prohibitively difficult. Training frontier AI models requires not just technical expertise but colossal datasets, immense compute resources, and access to advanced semiconductors—all of which are concentrated in a handful of countries. Even middle powers struggle to keep pace; for smaller states, self-sufficiency is largely impossible. This structural imbalance echoes the dependency theory of the twentieth century, which argued that industrialisation in the Global South was constrained by reliance on the industrial North. Today, the constraint is not factories and machines but GPUs and proprietary models.

The dependency trap also carries cultural and political implications. When algorithms designed in one cultural and political context are deployed globally, they encode specific assumptions about human behaviour, risk, and governance. For instance, content moderation algorithms on social media platforms often fail to capture the nuance of local languages or political contexts, leading to disproportionate censorship or neglect of harmful content. In Myanmar, Facebook's inability to adequately moderate hate speech in Burmese contributed to violence against the Rohingya. This was not merely a technical glitch but a reflection of dependency: the state lacked both the leverage and the alternatives to demand better safeguards. *Sovereignty is not just about where data resides but about whose values are inscribed into the systems that govern social life.*

Resistance to the dependency trap is emerging, but with mixed success. India has attempted to assert digital sovereignty by requiring data localisation and promoting domestic platforms. The European Union has pursued strict regulatory frameworks such as the GDPR and the proposed AI Act, aiming to set global standards. Yet smaller nations rarely have the market size or political clout to impose similar demands. For them, dependency often feels inevitable, a necessary cost of accessing modern technology. This resignation is precisely what entrenches the trap: the perception that there is no viable alternative leads to acceptance of terms that reinforce subordination.

Some observers argue that dependency may not be wholly negative, pointing out that smaller nations benefit from technology transfer, improved services, and integration into global markets. There is truth to this. AI-driven solutions can raise productivity, expand healthcare access, and enhance security in ways that local capacity alone could not achieve. Yet the crucial distinction lies in agency. Dependency becomes problematic not when tools are adopted, but when adoption forecloses the ability to shape, regulate, or even exit from those tools. A sovereign state should be able to choose its digital pathways; dependency traps emerge when choice narrows to compliance or exclusion.

The future may hold opportunities for reshaping these dynamics. Open-source AI initiatives, regional collaborations, and south-south partnerships could provide alternatives to wholesale reliance on Western or Chinese firms. Africa's nascent attempts to build continental AI strategies, or Latin America's experiments with shared digital infrastructure, represent early efforts at collective resistance. But these are fragile and underfunded compared to the industrial-scale investments of global superpowers. Without significant structural support, they risk being outpaced before they can mature.

The dependency trap is, therefore, not just a technical or economic issue but a defining question of global politics. It redraws the boundaries of sovereignty, determining which nations retain the capacity to steer their own futures and which are locked into technological vassalage. The irony is that smaller nations often recognise the risks but cannot afford to step aside; abstention from AI adoption risks marginalisation in global markets. Dependency is both the price of entry and the condition of participation. This paradox—between inclusion and autonomy, advancement and subordination—will shape the political economy of the twenty-first century.

The danger is not that smaller nations will be excluded from the AI revolution, but that they will be included only on terms that reinforce asymmetry. The dependency trap is not an accident of history but the predictable outcome of a system where the means of digital production are monopolised by a few and distributed to the many under conditions of control. For those caught within it, the question is not whether to participate but how to reclaim agency within an architecture designed to deny it.

Resistance and Reclamation

For centuries, empires thrived not only on the resources they extracted but also on the acquiescence of those from whom they extracted. The struggle over data has revived this dynamic in subtler but no less consequential ways. Unlike oil fields or mineral deposits, data is generated continuously by individuals, communities, and institutions—yet its ownership and control are far from evenly distributed. What distinguishes the twenty-first century is the emergence of conscious resistance. States and regions are beginning to craft legal and regulatory frameworks aimed at reclaiming sovereignty over digital resources. These efforts are ambitious, but they also reveal the profound structural limits of national control in a borderless digital economy. *The act of legislating against extraction is not simply about compliance; it is an assertion of identity and power in a world where data defines both.*

One of the most prominent attempts at reclamation has come from the European Union through the General Data Protection Regulation (GDPR), which came into force in 2018. Widely hailed as the most ambitious privacy law to date, GDPR sought to do more than protect individual rights—it attempted to recalibrate the global balance of power between tech corporations and democratic institutions. By imposing strict consent requirements, hefty fines for non-compliance, and rules about data portability, the EU positioned itself as the de facto global regulator. For multinational corporations, compliance with GDPR became unavoidable, given the size and value of the European market. In effect, Brussels managed to extend its regulatory reach beyond its borders, setting a benchmark that influenced data laws as far afield as Brazil's LGPD and California's CCPA. *This was digital sovereignty not as isolation, but as normative projection—the EU exporting its values outward rather than retreating inward.*

Yet GDPR's promise has also been tempered by its limits. Enforcement has been uneven, with smaller firms facing stricter scrutiny than the largest tech giants, who often have the legal and financial muscle to delay proceedings. Moreover, while GDPR raised the floor of privacy rights, it has not fundamentally altered the business model of surveillance capitalism. Targeted advertising remains dominant, and data remains concentrated in the hands of a few. The regulation has improved transparency, but it has not dismantled asymmetry. The lesson is clear: reclaiming sovereignty through law is possible, but the structural power of corporations means that resistance often translates into mitigation rather than transformation.

India represents another front in the movement toward reclamation, though through a different approach. With its Personal Data Protection Bill and subsequent localisation requirements, India has sought to keep its citizens' data within national borders. Policymakers framed localisation as a matter of national security, economic development, and strategic autonomy. The argument was straightforward: if Indian data is processed and stored abroad, it risks exploitation without benefit to the domestic economy. By mandating local storage, India hopes to spur domestic infrastructure investment, strengthen oversight, and prevent foreign monopolisation. *Data localisation, in this sense, is both a shield and a lever—a way of insulating the nation while nurturing local capability.*

But localisation, too, carries trade-offs. Critics argue that it risks fragmenting the internet, raising compliance costs for businesses, and creating obstacles for innovation. Smaller start-ups, in particular, may find localisation burdensome compared to global giants with resources to comply. Moreover, there are fears that localisation could empower states themselves to centralise surveillance. The Indian government's insistence on local storage may enhance sovereignty, but it simultaneously raises questions about whether sovereignty for the state comes at the expense of privacy for the individual. Resistance, in other words, may shift power away from corporations only to consolidate it within governments, creating new forms of dependency and coercion.

These efforts highlight the paradox of digital reclamation: the most ambitious attempts to claw back control operate within a system whose architecture inherently undermines territorial sovereignty. Data flows do not respect borders; algorithms evolve in transnational networks; and infrastructure supply chains are deeply globalised. Even nations with assertive policies face the reality that their autonomy is partial. India may store its data locally, but the chips powering its servers are still designed in the United States, manufactured in Taiwan, and dependent on global supply chains. The EU may legislate privacy, but its citizens still overwhelmingly rely on American platforms for communication and commerce. *Resistance can slow dependency, but it rarely severs it.*

Still, to dismiss these initiatives as futile would be to miss their deeper significance. They represent not merely regulatory manoeuvres but political statements about the nature of power in the digital age. GDPR asserted that the individual is not merely a data subject but a rights-bearing citizen. India's localisation laws declared that data is a national asset, akin to a strategic resource. Brazil's LGPD signalled that emerging economies could also shape norms rather than simply absorb them. Each initiative, however constrained, marks a refusal to accept the inevitability of extraction. The symbolic power of resistance can itself generate momentum, inspiring others to craft their own frameworks.

At the same time, reclamation efforts risk diverging into competing models of digital sovereignty. The EU's approach emphasises rights and regulation; India's stresses national control; China's model prioritises state dominance; the United States, for its part, leans on market-driven innovation with selective restrictions for strategic reasons. For smaller nations, navigating this fractured landscape is no simple matter. Aligning with one model may offer benefits but also deepens dependency on the sponsoring power. True reclamation requires not just resistance to external influence but collaboration across nations to articulate alternatives. Without such coordination, resistance risks being piecemeal and vulnerable to co-option.

Perhaps the most revealing aspect of these early efforts is that they reflect a broader philosophical struggle over the meaning of sovereignty itself. In a world where power is distributed through networks rather than borders, sovereignty cannot be understood as mere control over territory. It must encompass the capacity to set rules, enforce standards, and ensure accountability across transnational systems. GDPR's extraterritorial reach, India's localisation push, and Brazil's experiments all embody this reconceptualisation: sovereignty as a capacity to shape the rules of engagement in digital space. The challenge lies in making this capacity substantive rather than symbolic.

What emerges from these varied attempts is a spectrum of resistance—some aimed at constraining corporate power, others at asserting state prerogatives, and still others at shaping global norms. Each carries limitations, but together they mark the beginning of a global contest over who gets to define the terms of digital governance. The limits are stark, yet the alternatives to resistance are starker still: acquiescence, dependency, and the erosion of agency. Early reclamation may be imperfect, but it signals the recognition that sovereignty in the algorithmic age is not a passive inheritance—it is something to be actively defended, negotiated, and continually redefined.

Chapter 3

The Geopolitics of the Computer

Industrial might has always underpinned political power. In the nineteenth century, nations with shipyards and steel mills projected dominance across oceans and continents. In the twentieth century, oil refineries and nuclear plants became the nodes of strategic advantage, powering militaries, economies, and entire social orders. Today, the infrastructure that confers geopolitical weight is no longer forged in iron or fuelled by hydrocarbons. It is measured in compute—the capacity to process vast amounts of information, to run complex algorithms, to train artificial intelligence models whose sophistication determines both economic competitiveness and military preparedness. Semiconductor fabrication plants and hyperscale data centres are the new arms factories, and the nations that can command them will shape the trajectory of the twenty-first century.

The semiconductor industry epitomises this transformation. Chips are no longer simply components in consumer electronics; they are the lifeblood of advanced economies. Modern fighter jets, 5G networks, renewable energy grids, biomedical research, and financial systems all rely on chips designed with atomic-level precision. Yet the capacity to design and manufacture these semiconductors is concentrated in a handful of firms and countries. Taiwan's TSMC produces the world's most advanced logic chips, South Korea's Samsung competes closely, and the United States leads in design through companies like NVIDIA, AMD, and Qualcomm. But the supply chain is profoundly interdependent. Dutch firm ASML controls the production of extreme ultraviolet lithography machines—without which no cutting-edge chips can be manufactured—while Japanese firms dominate photoresists and specialised materials. *This web of dependency has created both extraordinary efficiency and extraordinary vulnerability, where a single choke point can destabilise global systems.*

The geopolitical implications of this concentration are starkest in the strategic competition between the United States and China. Washington recognises that control of the semiconductor supply chain is not merely a commercial issue but a national security imperative. Advanced chips power everything from artificial intelligence models to missile guidance systems. If Beijing gains unfettered access to the most advanced semiconductors, it narrows the technological and military gap with Washington. Consequently, the United States has imposed sweeping export controls on China, restricting access to high-end chips, design software, and the equipment required to manufacture them. These measures are unprecedented in their scope and signal the emergence of a new kind of technological containment strategy. For China, the stakes are existential: without access to advanced chips, its ambitions in AI, quantum computing, and military modernisation risk being throttled. Thus, semiconductors have become a flashpoint not merely of trade rivalry but of systemic rivalry, defining the contours of twenty-first-century great-power politics.

The metaphor of "chip wars" risks trivialising the complexity of the conflict. This is not a battle over tariffs or intellectual property theft alone. It is about who sets the pace of innovation and who dictates the rules of digital economies. The United States leverages choke points in the supply chain, while China accelerates investments in domestic semiconductor capacity, pouring billions into its "Made in China 2025" initiative. Yet China faces formidable obstacles: producing cutting-edge chips requires decades of accumulated expertise, global partnerships, and highly specialised equipment that cannot easily be replicated. The race, therefore, is not only technological but temporal: can China achieve self-sufficiency before U.S. restrictions significantly curtail its growth trajectory? The answer will shape not only the bilateral balance of power but also the global economic order.

If semiconductors are the hardware foundation of this struggle, cloud infrastructures are the operational layer that translates compute into usable power. Hyperscale data centres operated by Amazon Web Services, Microsoft Azure, and Google Cloud control a staggering share of global digital infrastructure. These platforms are not merely service providers; they are quasi-sovereign entities that establish the rules of access, dictate pricing, and determine the availability of computational resources to governments, corporations, and researchers alike. Their reach transcends borders: an African start-up may host its services on servers physically located in Ireland, governed by policies drafted in Seattle, and priced in U.S. dollars. This entanglement gives corporations a form of power once reserved for states: the ability to shape economic development, surveillance capacity, and even political stability in regions far from their headquarters.

The parallels with empire are instructive. Just as nineteenth-century empires controlled trade routes, ports, and supply chains, today's cloud providers control the arteries of the digital economy. States may regulate at the margins, but the gravitational pull of these infrastructures is immense. Even governments with ambitious localisation policies often rely on foreign clouds for scale, resilience, and advanced services. Control of compute is not only about capacity but about dependency, and dependency creates leverage. A nation dependent on foreign compute resources finds its sovereignty constrained in subtle but profound ways.

The emergence of these new power structures has created a widening global divide. Access to advanced compute is not evenly distributed. Wealthy nations and corporations can afford to train frontier AI models that require tens of thousands of specialised chips and consume megawatts of energy. By contrast, smaller economies find themselves limited to purchasing pre-trained models or leasing compute at high cost. This asymmetry locks nations into tiers of influence: the AI "haves," capable of shaping the trajectory of technology, and the AI "have-nots," forced to adapt to systems built elsewhere. The divide is not only economic but epistemic, determining who generates knowledge, who sets norms, and who reaps the economic and military dividends of advanced AI. *In effect, compute capacity has become a currency of power, stratifying the international system into new hierarchies of capability.*

The stakes of this divide extend beyond economics. Nations unable to access sufficient compute risk exclusion from the frontiers of biomedical research, climate modelling, financial innovation, and national defence. Their universities may lack the resources to conduct cutting-edge research, their firms may remain dependent on foreign models, and their governments may struggle to regulate technologies they do not fully understand. This dependency is not abstract; it translates into diminished bargaining power in international negotiations, vulnerability to external shocks, and reduced agency in shaping the digital future. In contrast, those with abundant compute resources can dictate standards, attract global talent, and project influence across borders.

Yet the geopolitics of compute is not solely about rivalry. It is also about the fragility of global interdependence. A disruption at a Taiwanese fab, a policy shift in Washington, or a cyberattack on a hyperscale data centre could ripple across continents, halting production lines, disrupting financial markets, and paralysing public services. Unlike oil, which can be stockpiled, compute cannot be easily hoarded. It is embedded in infrastructure, reliant on continuous supply chains, and bound by laws of physics that make scaling enormously complex. This fragility makes the geopolitics of compute not only a matter of strategic advantage but also of systemic risk.

The chapter that follows traces these dynamics in detail: how semiconductor fabrication plants have become the new battlegrounds of industrial policy; how the chip wars between Washington and Beijing reveal the vulnerabilities of global supply chains; how cloud infrastructures grant corporations state-like authority; and how the uneven distribution of compute is crystallising a global divide that will shape power relations for decades to come. To understand these developments is to grasp the new grammar of geopolitics, where power is increasingly defined not by the number of tanks in a nation's arsenal, but by the number of transistors on its chips and the scale of its data centres. Compute has become the substrate of twenty-first-century power, and its distribution will redraw the map of global influence.

The New Arms Factories

Power has always been built upon the ability to manufacture at scale. In the nineteenth century, the nations that controlled shipyards and steel mills determined the balance of naval strength, industrial reach, and colonial expansion. In the twentieth, oil refineries and nuclear plants became the linchpins of global influence, enabling modern warfare, mass mobility, and the industrialisation of entire societies. Today, the factories that underpin geopolitical power look very different. They are not vast furnaces pouring steel or docks assembling fleets of warships. They are semiconductor fabrication plants operating in cleanrooms smaller than a speck of dust, and hyperscale cloud infrastructures stretching silently across the globe. These facilities—immensely expensive, technologically sophisticated, and strategically indispensable—are the twenty-first century's equivalent of those older industrial arsenals. They determine which nations can train the most advanced artificial intelligence models, run the most complex simulations, and field the most capable digital economies. *Compute capacity has become the modern measure of geopolitical strength.*

Semiconductor fabs are the literal foundries of the digital age. Unlike past industries, where many nations could at least approximate the production of steel or oil, the production of cutting-edge chips is confined to an elite few. Taiwan Semiconductor Manufacturing Company (TSMC) and South Korea's Samsung stand at the summit of this hierarchy, producing chips at the three-nanometre level that are essential for frontier AI, military systems, and advanced consumer electronics. These fabs are both marvels of engineering and monuments to fragility. A single extreme ultraviolet lithography machine, built only by the Dutch firm ASML, costs more than $150 million and involves supply chains spanning dozens of countries. Constructing a state-of-the-art fab costs upwards of $20 billion and requires years of meticulous planning, as well as thousands of engineers versed in highly specialised domains. No state can casually replicate this capacity; it is the result of decades of incremental innovation and global interdependence. *This exclusivity transforms fabs from mere industrial sites into geopolitical assets as consequential as nuclear facilities.*

The concentration of these fabs in just a few territories has altered the geography of global politics. Taiwan, a self-governing island claimed by China, now finds its security intertwined with the world's reliance on its chipmaking capacity. The phrase "silicon shield" has entered strategic discourse: the notion that Taiwan's centrality to the semiconductor supply chain deters conflict, since any disruption would reverberate across industries worldwide. Yet the same reliance also sharpens the island's vulnerability, as both the United States and China manoeuvre to either protect or control this critical chokepoint. South Korea, too, finds itself balancing its role as a technological powerhouse with the risks of being caught in great-power rivalry. What emerges is not just competition over technology, but a remapping of strategic alliances and security doctrines around the defence of compute infrastructure.

If fabs are the hardware foundations of power, cloud infrastructures are the operational layer through which that power is exercised. Hyperscale data centres, operated primarily by American firms such as Amazon Web Services, Microsoft Azure, and Google Cloud, distribute compute resources globally. These centres are not warehouses of storage alone; they are the platforms on which modern economies run. Government databases, banking systems, health records, supply chains, and national security operations increasingly rely on the resilience and reach of these infrastructures. The ability to deliver compute on demand has become as critical to twenty-first-century governance as the ability to deliver electricity was in the last. Nations without access to these resources find themselves constrained not only in their technological ambitions but also in their sovereignty.

The dominance of a handful of corporations in this domain introduces a new dynamic: companies acting as de facto geopolitical actors. The location of a data centre, the pricing of cloud services, and the terms of service agreements carry implications far beyond the commercial. When Amazon or Microsoft decides to open a facility in a country, it alters that nation's digital landscape, enabling start-ups, reshaping labour markets, and shifting the balance of power between public and private sectors. Conversely, the withdrawal or denial of cloud services can cripple governments or firms. *Whereas shipyards once determined naval reach, today the control of cloud nodes determines digital reach.*

The analogy to steel mills is more than metaphorical. Just as steel production determined who could build railways, skyscrapers, and battleships, compute determines who can build advanced AI, process vast genomic datasets, or model the impacts of climate change. In both cases, control of the foundational capacity cascades into advantages across multiple domains. Military modernisation is a stark example. Training large-scale AI models requires enormous compute power; these models are now integral to cyber defence, intelligence analysis, autonomous systems, and the coordination of complex operations. The nations with access to advanced chips and cloud infrastructures thus possess a military edge comparable to that conferred by steel navies in earlier centuries.

Economic influence follows the same logic. Nations rich in compute capacity can accelerate innovation across sectors, from pharmaceuticals to finance, while those without remain dependent on external providers. This asymmetry creates new hierarchies. Countries with fabs and clouds set the pace of technological change; others adapt to their rules. The resulting dependency resembles older patterns of industrial dependence, where colonial powers exported raw materials and imported finished goods. Today, smaller nations export data and import compute, often at high cost and under conditions they cannot fully dictate. *This reinforces a global order in which compute-rich states consolidate wealth and power, while compute-poor states struggle to escape subordination.*

The costs of building these new arms factories underscore their strategic scarcity. Unlike steel mills, which could be scaled across many nations with sufficient capital and labour, semiconductor fabs demand extraordinary precision, often beyond the capacity of national industries. Similarly, hyperscale cloud infrastructures are not simply data warehouses; they require global networks, optimised energy sources, and economies of scale that few actors can achieve. This scarcity creates a paradox: compute is increasingly indispensable, yet access to it is increasingly unequal. In geopolitical terms, this is a combustible mix—high stakes combined with limited capacity—making control over these infrastructures one of the most contested domains of our time.

For the foreseeable future, semiconductor fabs and cloud infrastructures will remain the pivots around which technological power revolves. They are the arsenals of an age where influence is projected not through fleets or factories of steel, but through the invisible flows of computation. Nations that master these infrastructures consolidate their sovereignty and amplify their global voice. Those that cannot risk relegation to the periphery of technological modernity. Just as the industrial revolutions of the past determined the winners and losers of global order, the geopolitics of compute will determine the hierarchy of nations in the twenty-first century. To grasp this reality is to understand why fabs and clouds are not merely industries, but the new arms factories—factories that manufacture not weapons directly, but the very capacity to wield intelligence, security, and influence on a global scale.

The Chip Wars

Few commodities embody the paradox of modern globalisation as acutely as the semiconductor. These tiny slices of silicon, etched with billions of transistors smaller than a virus, form the foundation of the digital world. They power smartphones, supercomputers, fighter jets, cars, and the emerging arsenal of artificial intelligence applications. Yet despite their ubiquity, the supply chain that produces them is fragile, concentrated, and highly asymmetric. The contest over who controls their design, production, and distribution has become one of the defining geopolitical struggles of the twenty-first century. *The rivalry between the United States and China over semiconductors is not simply about commerce—it is about national security, technological supremacy, and the ability to project influence across the globe.*

The roots of this contest lie in the way semiconductors are produced. Unlike oil or steel, which can be extracted or manufactured within most industrial economies, advanced chips rely on an extraordinarily complex and globally distributed supply chain. The most sophisticated designs are often produced in the United States by firms such as NVIDIA, AMD, and

Qualcomm. The lithography machines necessary to etch circuits at the atomic scale are built exclusively by ASML in the Netherlands. Cutting-edge fabrication—the process of turning designs into physical chips—is dominated by Taiwan Semiconductor Manufacturing Company (TSMC) and, to a lesser degree, Samsung in South Korea. Japan produces critical photoresists and specialty chemicals. Together, this ecosystem creates a structure in which no single nation controls the entirety of production. But some nodes are so concentrated that they constitute *chokepoints*—if disrupted, entire industries could stall.

The United States has historically sat at the centre of this ecosystem, leveraging its dominance in design software, intellectual property, and advanced manufacturing equipment. American companies are indispensable, providing the architecture on which global chip production depends. But Washington also recognises the vulnerability inherent in this system, particularly the reliance on Taiwan. Any disruption to TSMC's output, whether from conflict, natural disaster, or economic coercion, would paralyse not only consumer electronics but also defence supply chains. For the United States, protecting and controlling the semiconductor industry has become a strategic imperative akin to maintaining control of oil routes in the twentieth century.

China, meanwhile, has long understood its dependence on foreign semiconductors as a strategic liability. Despite vast investment, Chinese firms remain years behind in producing chips at the most advanced nodes. Companies like SMIC (Semiconductor Manufacturing International Corporation) can fabricate at older scales suitable for less demanding applications, but they cannot yet match the performance of TSMC's or Samsung's latest products. This gap is not trivial: in artificial intelligence, military avionics, and high-performance computing, access to leading-edge chips determines what is technologically possible. For Beijing, achieving self-sufficiency in semiconductors is framed not merely as an industrial policy but as a matter of national survival in a world where sanctions can deny access to crucial technologies.

The United States has acted aggressively to preserve its lead. In 2019, the Trump administration placed Huawei, China's flagship technology firm, on an export blacklist, cutting it off from American-designed chips and software. More significantly, Washington leaned on allies to prevent TSMC from manufacturing advanced processors for Huawei, effectively crippling its smartphone business. This move demonstrated the immense leverage the United States could wield through control of semiconductor chokepoints. Under President Biden, these efforts intensified. Sweeping export controls announced in 2022 restricted China's access not only to advanced chips but also to the equipment and expertise necessary to produce them. These controls went beyond targeting individual firms; they represented an attempt to freeze China several generations behind the technological frontier.

China has not remained passive. Massive state-backed investment has flowed into domestic chipmaking initiatives, supported by policies such as the Made in China 2025 plan. Billions of dollars have been channelled into research and development, subsidies, and the recruitment of foreign talent. Success has been uneven. While China has achieved breakthroughs in certain areas, such as memory chips and less advanced logic nodes, it continues to struggle with the most sophisticated manufacturing steps. The reliance on ASML's extreme ultraviolet lithography machines, which remain inaccessible due to U.S. pressure, exemplifies how difficult it is to break free from entrenched supply chains. *The semiconductor industry resists brute-force replication; it demands patient accumulation of expertise across thousands of interdependent processes.*

This contest has reconfigured global alliances. The United States has pressed Japan, South Korea, and the Netherlands to align with its export restrictions, recognising that without their cooperation, controls would be porous. These countries face difficult choices. On the one hand, they benefit from close security ties with Washington and share concerns about Chinese technological dominance. On the other, China remains a vital trading partner, and cutting it off risks economic retaliation. South Korea's Samsung and SK Hynix, for instance, have significant facilities in China that serve global customers. Japan's materials firms rely heavily on exports to Chinese fabs. The semiconductor conflict thus places middle powers in an uncomfortable position, caught between the gravitational pulls of the world's two largest economies.

For China, this pressure has accelerated a turn toward what its leadership calls "dual circulation"—reducing dependence on external supply chains while strengthening domestic innovation. But achieving parity with global leaders may take decades, if it is achievable at all. Even partial success, however, could reshape the landscape. If China can close the gap in certain strategic areas, such as military applications or specialised AI chips, it may reduce the leverage Washington currently enjoys. The race, then, is not simply to dominate semiconductors outright but to deny the other side uncontested advantage.

The chip wars are not confined to the commercial or technological spheres. They shape military strategy. Modern weapons systems, from stealth aircraft to hypersonic missiles, depend on advanced chips for guidance, communication, and targeting. Artificial intelligence, increasingly central to military planning and cyber operations, requires vast compute power underpinned by cutting-edge semiconductors. The outcome of the U.S.–China rivalry in this domain will, therefore, influence the balance of power in both conventional and unconventional warfare. The analogy often drawn is to the nuclear arms race, but semiconductors differ in a crucial respect: they are not confined to arsenals but embedded in every aspect of society. This ubiquity makes their control more diffuse and their disruption potentially more catastrophic.

Philosophically, the semiconductor contest raises a deeper question about interdependence in an age of strategic rivalry. Globalisation produced a supply chain so finely tuned that it optimised for efficiency and cost at the expense of resilience. Now, as geopolitical fault lines widen, states are attempting to weaponise that interdependence. The result is a paradox: the very interconnectedness that made semiconductors possible is now a source of fragility and conflict. Whether the world fragments into competing blocs of semiconductor ecosystems, or finds a way to preserve some degree of shared infrastructure, will shape not only the future of technology but also the broader stability of international order.

What makes the chip wars a geopolitical flashpoint is not merely the competition itself but the impossibility of easy resolution. Unlike past industrial rivalries, where production could be localised with sufficient investment, semiconductors resist nationalisation. The precision required, the concentration of expertise, and the massive costs ensure that no country can dominate every stage. This creates a perpetual contest, where leverage is wielded through chokepoints and alliances rather than outright self-sufficiency. *The struggle over semiconductors is not a temporary trade dispute—it is the structural battlefield of twenty-first-century power.*

Infrastructure as Empire

Power today is not only measured in tanks, trade routes, or treaties. Increasingly, it is measured in who owns, controls, and governs the cloud. The infrastructure that stores data, runs applications, and connects billions of devices has become the nervous system of the global economy. What once looked like technical back-end services—server farms, undersea cables, content delivery networks—have morphed into levers of geopolitical influence. *To control the cloud is to set the rules of digital life, much as control of sea lanes or energy reserves once defined empire.*

The scale of this transformation is staggering. Just three corporations—Amazon Web Services, Microsoft Azure, and Google Cloud—command the vast majority of global cloud capacity. Their dominance is not confined to the United States; their data centres encircle the planet, from Dublin to Singapore, Sydney to São Paulo. Together, they provide the computing substrate upon which governments, militaries, banks, hospitals, and universities depend. Even state-led digital initiatives, from European e-government platforms to African fintech startups, often run on infrastructure leased from American tech giants. This asymmetry raises a profound question: what happens when private corporations wield a kind of infrastructural power once reserved for states?

Unlike traditional empires, which deployed armies and extracted tribute, today's infrastructural empires govern through code, contracts, and architecture. When AWS changes its terms of service, it can shape the viability of entire industries overnight. When Microsoft builds a new data centre region, it alters patterns of investment and digital dependency in that geography. When Google shifts its pricing model for AI services, start-ups across continents must recalibrate their strategies. The power is subtle but pervasive, operating less through decrees than through infrastructural choices that ripple across economies. The result is a quiet form of governance—law-like in its authority, but privately determined.

This power is not simply commercial. During the Russian invasion of Ukraine, Microsoft played a direct role in defending Ukraine's digital infrastructure, migrating government systems into the cloud to shield them from cyberattacks. Amazon delivered critical cybersecurity support, while SpaceX provided satellite connectivity through Starlink. These interventions, while celebrated as acts of support, reveal something unsettling: the defence of sovereign nations now depends on decisions made in corporate boardrooms. *Private companies are no longer neutral service providers; they are geopolitical actors whose infrastructures can alter the course of wars.*

The imperial analogy becomes sharper when considering how these platforms enforce their rules. States once imposed embargoes; now, cloud providers can unilaterally cut off access. Following Russia's invasion, many Western tech companies restricted their services to Russian customers. Beyond sanctions mandated by governments, companies like Google and Microsoft limited access to developer tools, cloud services, and even advertising platforms. For individuals and firms caught in the crossfire, the decision did not feel like a corporate choice but an act of sovereignty. The line between market discipline and geopolitical coercion is increasingly blurred.

This concentration of power also raises concerns of dependency. Nations eager to digitalise their economies often find themselves reliant on infrastructure owned abroad. Efforts to develop national clouds—such as France's "cloud de confiance" or China's state-backed cloud providers—reflect anxieties about ceding too much strategic autonomy to foreign corporations. Yet building cloud infrastructure at scale is prohibitively expensive, demanding not only capital but also expertise, ecosystems of developers, and trust from global clients. The paradox is clear: states want sovereignty in digital infrastructure, but the efficiency and ubiquity of private empires make autonomy elusive.

Philosophically, the cloud challenges how we think about borders. Data stored in a Dublin server may be owned by a Brazilian bank, accessed by a Kenyan developer, and regulated under U.S. law if the provider is American. Jurisdictional boundaries blur, replaced by overlapping spheres of corporate and state authority. This creates legal grey zones in which the rules of digital economies are set less by legislatures than by infrastructure providers. Scholars describe this as "lex informatica"—the law embedded in code and architecture. In practice, it means that AWS or Azure may enforce stricter privacy or security standards than certain governments, effectively creating private law with global reach.

The comparison to historical empires is not metaphorical flourish. Consider the British Empire's reliance on maritime dominance. Controlling shipping lanes allowed Britain not just to move goods but to dictate who could trade with whom, under what terms. Today, cloud providers are building private equivalents of these maritime routes—undersea fibre cables owned and operated not by states but by tech companies. Google's "Equiano" cable runs along Africa's west coast; Facebook's "2Africa" project will encircle the continent. Control of these arteries means control over digital connectivity, bandwidth pricing, and the strategic direction of emerging markets. *Infrastructure is empire because it shapes the very conditions of participation in the digital economy.*

Critics warn that such concentrated power entrenches inequalities. Smaller nations may find themselves unable to negotiate favourable terms or enforce domestic regulations against multinational providers. The asymmetry is not unlike that faced by colonies negotiating with imperial powers: formal sovereignty remains, but practical autonomy is constrained. Some governments respond with data localisation laws, requiring that data about their citizens be stored domestically. Others pursue regional collaborations, as the European Union has attempted with projects like GAIA-X. Yet these efforts often struggle against the gravitational pull of efficiency, cost, and scale that global providers offer.

The corporations themselves, aware of their growing scrutiny, attempt to frame their role as custodians rather than rulers. They emphasise commitments to transparency, sustainability, and compliance with local laws. Yet their sheer indispensability complicates the narrative. Governments can regulate, but they cannot easily replace or bypass these infrastructures. Even China, which has invested heavily in domestic cloud providers like Alibaba Cloud, recognises the challenge of competing globally with the reach of American firms. The reality is that in many regions, the empire of infrastructure is not chosen but accepted as a default.

What makes this development particularly consequential is its durability. Unlike consumer platforms, which can rise and fall with shifting user preferences, infrastructure embeds itself deeply. Once a government ministry or hospital system migrates its operations to AWS, switching becomes costly, complex, and politically fraught. Dependency hardens over time, locking nations into arrangements where private corporations function as enduring gatekeepers. This stickiness mirrors historical patterns: railways, telegraphs, and ports once entrenched imperial influence in ways that persisted long after political winds shifted.

The rise of cloud empires invites reflection on sovereignty itself. If sovereignty once meant control over territory and resources, today it increasingly involves control over data flows, algorithms, and compute capacity. Yet sovereignty exercised through corporate infrastructures is inherently different: it is contractual, revocable, and fragmented. A government can nationalise a factory; it cannot as easily nationalise a dispersed network of global data centres. *The new empire is harder to see, harder to challenge, and perhaps harder to escape.*

Still, the story is not one of unchallenged corporate dominance. Nations are experimenting with hybrid approaches—building strategic domestic capacity while maintaining pragmatic ties to global providers. Alliances between states and corporations are also deepening, as seen in defence contracts awarded to cloud firms or joint ventures in emerging markets. The contest is not over whether infrastructure should be empire, but over who commands it and under what terms. The coming decades will likely see a rebalancing, with some regions carving out greater autonomy, others doubling down on integration, and corporations themselves navigating the pressures of regulation, competition, and geopolitics.

The empire of infrastructure is not an accident of technology but a deliberate concentration of capital, expertise, and control. It represents a structural shift in how power is organised and exercised in the twenty-first century. To grasp it fully requires seeing past the familiar language of markets and services, recognising instead that what is at stake is governance—who decides the rules by which digital economies operate, and who enforces them. The answer, increasingly, is not states alone. It is the corporations that own the servers, cables, and platforms on which the world now runs.

The Great Divide

The defining scarcity of the artificial intelligence age is not data, nor algorithms, but compute. While data is abundant and algorithms can circulate freely through open-source communities, the raw computational power needed to train frontier models remains tightly concentrated. This scarcity has profound implications. Access to high-performance computing resources increasingly determines not just who can innovate but who can govern, who can secure, and who can influence. *The divide between those who control vast computational capacity and those who do not is fast becoming one of the most consequential lines of separation in global politics.*

The training of state-of-the-art AI systems now requires staggering volumes of processing power, measured in the millions or even billions of dollars' worth of specialised chips. For example, training OpenAI's GPT-4 reportedly demanded tens of thousands of cutting-edge GPUs running for months, consuming enough electricity to power a small town. These costs and infrastructure requirements are far beyond the reach of most governments, let alone universities or startups. In practice, only a handful of nations—the United States, China, and to a lesser extent a few advanced economies in Europe and Asia—command the resources necessary to build and operate such systems at scale. For others, participation is mediated through dependence, often reliant on foreign corporations or alliances to access even modest levels of compute.

This asymmetry is producing a new form of digital stratification. At the top tier sit countries and companies with direct access to advanced semiconductor manufacturing, cloud hyperscalers, and the capital to sustain large-scale AI development. These are the *AI haves*, whose control of compute allows them to shape the frontier of innovation and, by extension, the rules of the global digital economy. Below them are the *AI have-nots*, nations excluded from this core club and increasingly locked into roles as consumers rather than producers of AI technology. The divide is not absolute—many middle powers can adapt AI tools for domestic use—but their ability to influence the trajectory of AI, to set ethical norms, or to secure technological sovereignty remains constrained by dependency on foreign compute.

The strategic consequences are immense. Consider healthcare. Nations with access to advanced AI can develop predictive diagnostic models, accelerate drug discovery, and integrate personalised medicine into their systems. Those without must wait for such innovations to be commercialised by others, often at costs and under conditions they cannot control. In agriculture, AI-rich countries can deploy precision farming at scale, while others remain vulnerable to food insecurity exacerbated by climate change. In defence, the gap is even more pronounced: the ability to train autonomous systems, simulate battlefield scenarios, or process massive streams of intelligence data is contingent on compute power. Without it, states are relegated to second-order status, dependent on alliances for technologies critical to their national security.

This hierarchy is not unprecedented. In the nineteenth century, the ability to harness industrial capacity divided nations into great powers and dependent states. Shipyards, steel mills, and railways marked the difference between empires and colonies. In the twentieth century, nuclear weapons became the ultimate arbiter of strategic influence, creating a sharp divide between nuclear and non-nuclear powers. Today, the possession of compute capacity—vast arrays of advanced semiconductors, high-bandwidth interconnections, and colossal energy-hungry data centres—functions as the new determinant of influence. Unlike nuclear technology, which spread only slowly, AI systems built on compute diffuse rapidly through digital platforms, exacerbating the imbalance.

Some argue that cloud computing could bridge this divide, allowing nations without domestic infrastructure to "rent" compute from global providers. In practice, however, this creates dependencies of a different kind. Renting access does not equate to sovereignty. Contracts can be altered, access can be cut, and the most advanced systems are often restricted by export controls or pricing structures designed to protect strategic advantage. A nation reliant on foreign cloud services for its AI capabilities may find itself vulnerable to political pressures or commercial priorities it cannot control. *Access without autonomy is dependency by another name.*

The United States has recognised this dynamic and acted to preserve its lead through semiconductor export controls. By restricting China's ability to acquire high-end GPUs and chipmaking equipment, Washington seeks to slow Beijing's advance in AI. These measures underscore how compute is no longer seen as a neutral commercial good but as a strategic resource akin to oil or uranium. China, for its part, has doubled down on efforts to develop indigenous chip capabilities, though the complexity of semiconductor supply chains means catching up may take years, if not decades. In the meantime, the gap between the U.S. and China on the one hand, and the rest of the world on the other, only widens.

Europe offers another perspective. Despite world-class research institutions and a strong regulatory apparatus, Europe lacks a hyperscaler of its own to rival Amazon, Microsoft, or Google. Its initiatives, such as the GAIA-X project, aim to build a federated cloud infrastructure, but progress has been uneven. The continent risks becoming a rule-maker without being a technology-shaper—able to legislate on AI ethics and privacy but unable to anchor those rules in domestic infrastructure. For developing nations, the prospects are starker still. Without significant investment or regional alliances, many may never achieve meaningful AI sovereignty, instead becoming perpetual clients of external providers.

This divide also raises questions of justice. If AI is to transform fields as essential as education, healthcare, and climate modelling, then the unequal distribution of compute power threatens to deepen global inequalities. The benefits of AI may accrue disproportionately to wealthy nations, while poorer countries remain excluded or dependent. Philosophically, this invites reflection on the idea of a "technological commons." Should compute be treated as a global public good, accessible to all in pursuit of shared human progress? Or is it destined to remain a scarce resource hoarded by those with the capital and industrial capacity to control it?

Pragmatism suggests that complete egalitarianism is unlikely. The costs of frontier compute are so high that only a few actors can realistically sustain them. Yet there may be intermediate paths. International collaborations, regional compute-sharing initiatives, or global funding mechanisms could allow a broader base of nations to access at least part of the benefits. Just as nuclear power was channelled through frameworks like the International

Atomic Energy Agency, so too might compute be partially socialised, with governance structures to ensure access while limiting risks. But such arrangements require trust, coordination, and political will that remain elusive in an era of sharpening geopolitical rivalry.

The more immediate concern is the solidification of tiers of influence. Once entrenched, the divide becomes self-reinforcing. Nations with compute lead in AI research, which generates wealth, talent, and further investment in compute, perpetuating their dominance. Nations without struggle to break into this virtuous cycle, lacking the infrastructure to attract talent or the scale to compete. Over time, this dynamic may harden into a digital caste system: a handful of AI superpowers, a group of middle-tier adopters, and a long tail of dependent users.

What distinguishes this divide from earlier technological inequalities is its invisibility. The lack of access to compute is not as tangible as the absence of factories or weapons. It manifests instead in slower innovation cycles, reduced competitiveness, and diminished bargaining power in global forums. Yet its effects are no less profound. In a world increasingly governed by AI systems—from trade flows to military strategies—the inability to shape those systems amounts to a loss of agency on the world stage.

Ultimately, the great divide in compute access is not just a technical issue but a political and moral one. It forces societies to ask whether power should be concentrated in the hands of a few or distributed more widely. It challenges the international system to confront the reality that sovereignty in the twenty-first century may hinge not on land or resources but on the ability to command the invisible infrastructure of intelligence itself. *Those who have compute will shape the future; those who do not will live in it on terms set by others.*

Chapter 4

Algorithms as Weapons of Influence

Power has always been tied to the ability to shape perception. From the pamphleteers of the Reformation to the broadcast networks of the twentieth century, the forces that command attention have determined the direction of societies. What distinguishes our present age is not the existence of propaganda or political persuasion—these are as old as politics itself—but the degree to which influence has been automated, scaled, and personalised through algorithms. *Artificial intelligence does not merely transmit messages; it curates realities, tailoring entire worlds of information to the susceptibilities of each individual.* This shift has turned the information environment itself into a contested battlefield, one in which the boundaries between truth, manipulation, and collective imagination are increasingly difficult to discern.

The rise of AI-driven disinformation has shown how fragile the assumptions underpinning democratic life truly are. A doctored video, a fabricated news story, or a swarm of automated social media accounts can ripple outward with destabilising effect, undermining trust in institutions and sowing confusion in public debate. Deepfake technology exemplifies this disruption: a convincing video of a leader announcing a policy shift, broadcast even briefly before being debunked, can trigger market reactions, diplomatic crises, or public unrest. *The mere possibility that any piece of content could be fake injects a corrosive scepticism into the civic sphere.* Democracies depend on citizens' ability to deliberate on a shared foundation of facts; when that foundation is systematically eroded, governance itself falters. Authoritarian regimes, by contrast, often thrive in conditions of manufactured uncertainty, using information chaos to consolidate control and to discredit dissent.

Equally consequential is the subtler influence of algorithmic recommendation systems. These systems do not announce themselves as propaganda, yet their effects can be more profound than overt disinformation campaigns. By privileging some content over others, recommendation engines on platforms like YouTube, TikTok, and Facebook effectively shape the horizons of what citizens see, know, and discuss. The logic of maximising engagement drives these systems toward amplification of content that evokes strong emotional responses—anger, outrage, fear—creating feedback loops that intensify polarisation. When an algorithm quietly nudges millions of people toward certain narratives, the line between organic political mobilisation and engineered sentiment blurs. *The fate of elections, the organisation of protests, and even the endurance of democratic norms are increasingly mediated by systems designed not to inform but to optimise attention.*

This phenomenon represents a profound evolution of propaganda itself. During the Cold War, influence campaigns relied on broadcast technologies, leaflets, and carefully crafted radio programmes. They sought to win "hearts and minds" through the blunt tools of one-to-many communication. Today, propaganda operates on a far more granular scale. AI-driven systems can target individuals with personalised messages, test their resonance in real time, and adapt strategies dynamically. Virality is no longer an accidental feature of information flow but a weaponised objective. States and political actors exploit these dynamics to seed narratives that appear grassroots, yet are algorithmically amplified. Unlike the propaganda wars of the past, which unfolded across borders with clear lines of ideological confrontation, today's influence campaigns seep into the intimate spaces of everyday life—social feeds, private chats, search queries—where persuasion is most difficult to detect and resist.

The cumulative effect of these dynamics is a growing crisis of trust. When every image can be fabricated, every news item questioned, and every viral trend suspected of manipulation, societies risk entering a condition of epistemic fatigue. Citizens no longer know what information to believe, nor which sources to trust. Some retreat into cynicism, assuming all political communication is manipulation. Others cling to partisan echo chambers, mistaking alignment with their own biases for truth. The result is fragmentation: instead of a shared public sphere, democracies fracture into isolated communities of belief, each with its own "facts." Governance in such conditions becomes not merely difficult but perilous, as legitimacy itself erodes when institutions can no longer command broad trust.

The stakes are not limited to elections or political stability. Markets too are vulnerable to algorithmic influence, as traders react to signals that may have been manipulated. Social movements can be accelerated or discredited through the viral spread of fabricated content. Even international diplomacy can be disrupted, with adversaries exploiting AI-driven campaigns to test red lines, foment discord, or erode alliances. The battlefield is not geographic but cognitive; the objective is not territorial conquest but narrative dominance. *In such an environment, power belongs not only to those who wield military force or economic leverage, but to those who can control the flows of perception itself.*

What makes this chapter urgent is the recognition that algorithms are no longer neutral conduits of information. They are active agents of influence, shaping how billions interpret reality. Their designers may not have set out to build propaganda machines, yet by aligning incentives with attention, they have created infrastructures that authoritarian regimes and opportunistic actors can weaponise with remarkable efficiency. Democracies face a paradox: the same open systems that allow for vibrant expression and innovation also render them acutely vulnerable to manipulation. Protecting free speech while mitigating algorithmic distortion presents one of the defining governance challenges of the twenty-first century.

The reader should not mistake this for a story of technological determinism. Algorithms do not operate in a vacuum; they reflect political choices, economic incentives, and societal values. Yet the scale and speed with which they now operate have shifted the balance of agency. A pamphlet could persuade; a broadcast could mobilise; but an AI-driven influence system can micro-target millions simultaneously, adjusting tactics at machine speed. This raises profound questions about autonomy, responsibility, and the possibility of collective deliberation in conditions of pervasive manipulation.

This chapter will trace how AI has turned influence into a weapon as consequential as any traditional instrument of power. It will examine the rise of disinformation and deepfakes, the quiet but profound sway of recommendation algorithms, the transformation of propaganda into a personalised, algorithmically-driven enterprise, and the destabilising effects of widespread distrust. Together, these forces illuminate how the struggle for power in the twenty-first century is increasingly fought not on battlefields or in boardrooms, but in the contested space of perception. *To understand algorithms as weapons of influence is to grasp how the architecture of information itself has become a central axis of global competition, reshaping the conditions of democracy, governance, and human agency.*

The Information Battlefield

Power in the twenty-first century is increasingly measured not only in economic or military terms, but in the ability to shape perceptions of reality itself. The struggle over information has become a central arena of geopolitical competition, and artificial intelligence has transformed the weapons available. The tools of persuasion and propaganda that once relied on mass broadcasting have given way to algorithmically enhanced campaigns of disinformation, deepfake manipulation, and sentiment engineering. *What makes this moment distinct is not the existence of falsehood, but the industrial scale and forensic precision with which it can now be produced, distributed, and optimised.* Democracies, with their reliance on informed citizens and open debate, find themselves uniquely vulnerable to these attacks, while authoritarian states often see opportunity in exploiting informational chaos to tighten their grip.

Disinformation has always been a feature of politics, but the AI age has changed its economics. Creating a convincing fake used to demand expertise, resources, and time. Today, generative models can fabricate news articles, forge voices, and produce photo-realistic images or videos within minutes. What was once the domain of intelligence services is now within reach of fringe political groups, commercial actors, or even individuals with minimal technical skill. The low barrier to entry means the volume of false or misleading content has expanded exponentially, overwhelming fact-checking institutions and eroding the capacity of societies to distinguish between credible and fraudulent sources. *Information warfare has become democratised, but with consequences that most democracies are unprepared to absorb.*

Deepfakes illustrate this acceleration starkly. Early examples were crude, uncanny imitations. Now they can capture subtle facial expressions, replicate vocal cadence, and generate persuasive video evidence that can fool not just the public but also sophisticated detection systems. A deepfake of a Ukrainian president surrendering during the Russian invasion in 2022 was quickly debunked, yet its brief circulation underscored the threat: even if exposed as false, the disruption and doubt it introduces can serve its purpose. Financial markets, already hypersensitive to signals, are another domain of vulnerability. A convincing video of a CEO announcing bankruptcy, spread virally for a matter of hours, could trigger economic chaos before corrections reach the same scale. *The most dangerous aspect of deepfakes may not be their success in convincing, but their success in making truth itself implausible.*

Alongside disinformation and deepfakes is the more insidious phenomenon of sentiment manipulation. Algorithms that once recommended music or books now refine their ability to map human psychology at scale. By analysing social media behaviour—likes, shares, pauses in scrolling—they infer emotional states with startling accuracy. These inferences can be weaponised to deliver tailored content designed to trigger outrage, fear, or solidarity depending on the strategic objective. Political operatives no longer rely on broad messages aimed at entire electorates; instead, they micro-target individuals or groups, nudging their beliefs and behaviours with surgical precision. The Cambridge Analytica scandal offered a glimpse of how data-driven political influence might be mobilised. The sophistication of today's AI systems takes this far beyond personality-based advertising, into a realm where *the subconscious levers of emotion are continually pulled by unseen hands.*

For democracies, the danger lies in their openness. Free media ecosystems, plural political debate, and the high value placed on individual expression create fertile ground for manipulation. Disinformation spreads not in spite of democratic freedoms, but because of them. Attempts to regulate content risk accusations of censorship, fuelling further distrust. Authoritarian states, by contrast, use these dynamics asymmetrically. They deploy AI-driven campaigns abroad to weaken adversaries, while tightly controlling information at home to limit reciprocal vulnerabilities. Russia's use of coordinated disinformation during Western elections and China's efforts to shape narratives around issues like Hong Kong protests or Xinjiang policies highlight how authoritarian regimes weaponise the informational openness of democracies while insulating themselves against external critique.

The effects extend beyond politics into the very fabric of civic life. Trust, once eroded, is not easily restored. When populations begin to assume that any piece of information may be false or manipulated, cynicism becomes a default posture. This "liar's dividend"—the ability of genuine wrongdoers to dismiss authentic evidence as fake—further destabilises governance. Courts, journalists, and watchdog institutions find themselves paralysed when video or audio evidence can be plausibly denied. Public debate shifts from deliberation over policies to endless argument about whether the underlying facts can be trusted. *The cost is not simply confusion but paralysis: the inability of societies to act collectively because they cannot agree on what is real.*

There are, however, competing perspectives on the scale of this threat. Some scholars argue that the panic over disinformation exaggerates its impact, noting that traditional media, partisan identities, and economic conditions remain stronger drivers of political behaviour than online manipulation. They point out that while disinformation circulates widely, it does not always translate into persuasion or behavioural change. Yet even if the direct influence of any single campaign is overstated, the cumulative effect of pervasive doubt is undeniable. The goal is not always to convert but to confuse, to exhaust the public's capacity to discern, and to weaken the shared foundations on which democratic legitimacy rests. *Even scepticism, when weaponised, becomes a powerful instrument of control.*

What distinguishes AI-enabled manipulation from previous forms of propaganda is its adaptability. Messages can be A/B tested at scale, iterated in real time, and fine-tuned for maximum impact. Feedback loops between user behaviour and algorithmic output mean that influence campaigns evolve dynamically, without the need for centralised orchestration. This makes them harder to trace and counteract, as disinformation mutates to exploit emergent cultural fissures or shifting political climates. The battlefield is not static; it is algorithmically alive, responding at machine speed to human vulnerabilities.

In this environment, defending democratic integrity requires more than technical detection of false content. It requires a rethinking of resilience: how to build publics capable of navigating uncertainty without descending into nihilism. Some propose bolstering media literacy, teaching citizens to approach all information critically. Others argue for structural reforms of platform incentives, holding companies accountable for systems that privilege engagement over accuracy. Still others emphasise international cooperation, as disinformation campaigns rarely respect borders. Each of these approaches acknowledges that the challenge is not merely technological but institutional, cultural, and political.

The information battlefield, then, is not simply a matter of fake news or fraudulent videos. It is a systemic struggle over the conditions of belief in the digital age. *The capacity to generate, circulate, and manipulate narratives at scale has become a decisive factor in global power.* Democracies, built on the fragile premise that truth can be collectively pursued and agreed upon, face an existential challenge when that premise is persistently undermined. Authoritarian regimes, conversely, exploit these dynamics to destabilise their rivals while reinforcing their own legitimacy at home. To understand AI's role in this contest is to recognise that the frontline of power today is not only geographical or economic, but cognitive. Those who can command attention and manipulate perception wield influence as profound as any military arsenal.

Shaping Reality

Few forces in contemporary life are as quietly powerful as the algorithms that curate what we see and hear each day. They do not shout their influence, nor do they announce themselves as arbiters of truth or importance. Instead, they work silently, ordering the chaos of information into feeds, recommendations, and trending topics that feel organic but are in fact computationally sculpted. *The power of these systems lies not in overt manipulation, but in the subtle shaping of attention itself.* What we do not see is as important as what we do, and what we repeatedly encounter gradually becomes the common sense of a digital public sphere.

Recommendation engines began as tools of convenience—helping users navigate vast libraries of books, music, or films. Yet as social media platforms became the dominant channel for news and political discourse, these same mechanisms came to play a far more consequential role. They determine not just what products are consumed but which stories rise to prominence, which grievances are amplified, and which leaders are elevated or undermined. In effect, they *distribute visibility as a scarce resource.* A political speech or protest video buried in the algorithm might as well not exist; another, pushed to millions of screens, can ignite nationwide mobilisation.

The evidence of algorithmic influence on elections is no longer speculative. In the 2016 United States presidential race, Facebook's recommendation systems were found to have amplified inflammatory content at rates far higher than neutral reporting, because outrage proved more engaging. Internal documents later revealed that the company understood how its algorithms rewarded polarisation yet hesitated to reform them, fearing decreased engagement. Similarly, during Brazil's 2018 election, WhatsApp—owned by Meta—was flooded with targeted misinformation campaigns, whose virality was supercharged by the platform's forwarding features. The recommendation logic was not neutral; it privileged content most likely to spread, regardless of accuracy. *In doing so, it reshaped political discourse by privileging emotional contagion over deliberative debate.*

Elections are not the only sites of impact. Protest movements, too, are born and sustained through algorithmic visibility. The Arab Spring uprisings were often narrated as "Twitter revolutions," but closer analysis shows the decisive role of recommendation dynamics in spreading footage and testimony across borders. Hashtags that gained algorithmic momentum helped coordinate collective action, while others were suppressed or sidelined. More recently, the Black Lives Matter protests in 2020 gained global reach partly because recommendation systems elevated visceral video evidence of police violence, ensuring that outrage could not be confined to local contexts. Algorithms turned private suffering into public spectacle, and from that spectacle emerged solidarity and mobilisation. Yet the same systems can just as easily suppress dissent, as seen in the selective visibility of pro-democracy content within China's digital ecosystems, where algorithms are tuned to privilege state narratives and downplay resistance.

The mechanism of influence is rarely straightforward propaganda. Instead, it lies in the subtle biases of curation. Recommendation engines are optimised for engagement, not truth. They privilege the sensational over the sober, the divisive over the nuanced, the emotionally charged over the complex. This does not mean they invent falsehoods wholesale, but that they create an environment where extreme content thrives disproportionately. Over time, this shifts the centre of political discourse. *What people believe to be the mainstream consensus is itself a function of what the algorithm repeatedly presents as popular, trending, or urgent.* Reality becomes algorithmically normalised.

There is an irony here: most users perceive their feeds as personalised mirrors of their interests, when in fact they are seeing the outcome of opaque optimisation processes. The feedback loop is seductive. Users click on what resonates, algorithms learn and refine, and the resulting stream of content increasingly conforms to—and exaggerates—existing predispositions. This is not manipulation in the sense of implanting foreign ideas but rather amplification: feeding back to individuals the strongest versions of their biases until those biases appear as undeniable truths. The formation of collective beliefs under such conditions is less about persuasion and more about reinforcement. *Societies fracture not because new ideologies emerge but because existing divisions are sharpened to knife edges by algorithmic feedback.*

There are defenders of algorithmic systems who argue that they simply reflect human preferences—that outrage circulates because people want it, not because platforms force it upon them. Yet this perspective underestimates the engineering of choice. When billions of posts exist, the selection of a few to place at the top of a feed is already a profound act of power. That power is wielded by algorithms designed not to reflect society but to maximise commercial outcomes. Moreover, the opacity of these systems denies citizens the ability to scrutinise or contest how their information environments are shaped. What masquerades as neutral technology is, in practice, an infrastructure of influence.

The geopolitical consequences are far-reaching. Authoritarian regimes, observing the influence of recommendation systems, have moved to weaponise them directly. Russia's state-sponsored media outlets exploit algorithms on YouTube and Facebook to seed divisive narratives abroad, knowing that polarising content will be algorithmically privileged. China, meanwhile, has cultivated its own domestic platforms with recommendation engines aligned to state priorities, creating parallel realities for domestic and international audiences. The West, by contrast, relies heavily on private corporations to moderate and configure the information landscape, leaving democratic societies exposed to manipulation not only from foreign adversaries but also from the profit motives of their own companies.

At a deeper philosophical level, the rise of algorithmic recommendation systems poses a challenge to the very notion of a shared public sphere. Political theorists from Habermas onward have emphasised the importance of a common space for rational deliberation, however imperfect. Algorithms fragment that space into countless micro-publics, each seeing different versions of reality. The result is not only polarisation but epistemic disorientation: a loss of confidence that neighbours, colleagues, or even family members are seeing the same world. In such conditions, compromise becomes nearly impossible. *When reality itself appears fractured, collective governance frays.*

There are those who view algorithmic influence with more optimism, pointing to cases where personalised recommendations have connected citizens to diverse perspectives or marginalised voices. For example, recommendation systems have helped indigenous activists gain global visibility and enabled niche political movements to coordinate across borders. Yet the problem lies in scale and asymmetry. For every example of empowerment, there are countless instances where outrage or extremism gained disproportionate reach. The design of these systems ensures that positive outcomes are exceptions rather than the rule.

As societies wrestle with the political implications of algorithmic curation, debates have emerged over responsibility. Should platforms be held accountable for the content they promote, or are they merely intermediaries reflecting user behaviour? Should governments intervene to regulate recommendation systems, and if so, how without veering into censorship? These are not technical questions alone; they are questions about sovereignty, legitimacy, and the architecture of democratic life. *The quiet power of algorithms is that they set the terms of debate before debate even begins.*

In recognising the influence of recommendation systems, one must also grapple with the difficulty of resisting them. Human cognition is ill-suited to resist constant nudges delivered with precision timing. Outrage captures attention because it taps primal instincts; repetition breeds familiarity; familiarity breeds belief. Even the most sceptical citizen is not immune to the cumulative effects of exposure. Efforts to "just think critically" underestimate the structural asymmetry between human psychology and machine-optimised persuasion. It is not enough to encourage individual vigilance when the very architecture of attention is algorithmically manipulated.

The shaping of reality through algorithms is perhaps the most consequential yet least visible transformation of political life in the twenty-first century. Elections, protests, and public opinion no longer emerge from the raw aggregation of citizen voices but from streams curated, ranked, and optimised by machines. *To understand politics today requires understanding not just who speaks, but who is heard, and why.* Those who design and control recommendation systems wield influence comparable to that of statesmen, media barons, or religious leaders of the past. Yet unlike those figures, they often operate with limited accountability, their power exercised in code rather than proclamations. The struggle over this new terrain of influence will determine not only the future of democracy but the very conditions under which societies can agree on what is true, what matters, and what is worth acting upon.

Propaganda 2.0

During the Cold War, the struggle between East and West was fought not only through nuclear brinkmanship and proxy wars, but also through words, images, and ideas. The United States broadcast Voice of America into Soviet territories, while Radio Moscow targeted audiences abroad with carefully crafted narratives. Pamphlets, films, and staged cultural exchanges became tools of persuasion. Propaganda was about *narrative supremacy*—a battle over which version of reality would be believed, both at home and abroad. What distinguishes the present is not the existence of propaganda, but its unprecedented velocity, reach, and precision, all driven by algorithms optimised for virality. States no longer need to push their messages via leaflets or clandestine broadcasts; they can seed disinformation in digital ecosystems where algorithms themselves ensure that the most provocative narratives rise to the surface.

The Cold War model of propaganda was essentially broadcast-centric. Governments projected their messages outward, hoping they would resonate and ripple through society. Success depended on capturing attention through state media or infiltrating the editorial priorities of rival newsrooms. The difficulty lay in scale: reaching millions required enormous infrastructure and sustained investment. Today, however, scale is inherent. Social media platforms have engineered systems where information distribution is frictionless. A single video uploaded by a state-backed account or anonymous troll can, if the algorithm detects engagement potential, be recommended to millions overnight. *The infrastructure of virality has democratised influence, allowing even modestly resourced actors to punch far above their weight.*

Consider Russia's influence campaigns around the 2016 US presidential election. Rather than relying on overt propaganda outlets, operatives at the Internet Research Agency posed as ordinary Americans, creating divisive content that was deliberately designed to exploit existing fractures—race, immigration, guns, and religion. The strategy was not to persuade people of a wholly new worldview, but to amplify existing grievances until they dominated political conversation. Algorithms, tuned to maximise engagement, elevated these emotionally charged posts, ensuring they spread more effectively than sober reporting. The brilliance of this approach lay in its indirectness: rather than broadcasting the Kremlin's narrative, it encouraged Americans to argue amongst themselves, each side convinced it was defending truth against manipulation. The Cold War's ideological clash of systems gave way to a postmodern chaos in which *the line between propaganda and organic discourse became nearly impossible to discern.*

China has developed its own model of Propaganda 2.0, more systematic and less chaotic. Its "Great Firewall" controls domestic flows of information, while platforms like WeChat and Douyin curate reality in ways that align with state interests. Yet China has also learned to weaponise virality abroad. State-backed accounts seed content on Twitter and YouTube designed to shape perceptions of issues such as Xinjiang, Taiwan, or Hong Kong. What distinguishes Chinese campaigns is their blending of soft power with algorithmic exploitation: polished videos presenting China as a benevolent modern power are circulated alongside discrediting narratives about Western hypocrisy. Here, virality is harnessed not only for disruption but also for image-building, a twenty-first century analogue to Cold War cultural diplomacy, but executed with algorithmic amplification.

The logic of Propaganda 2.0 differs profoundly from its Cold War predecessor. Where the latter sought to persuade mass audiences with coherent ideological narratives, today's influence campaigns often aim at disorientation. Disinformation spreads not by offering a single alternative truth but by flooding the environment with competing claims, sowing doubt about the very possibility of truth itself. A deepfake video need not be widely believed to be effective; its mere existence creates uncertainty, eroding confidence in authentic sources. *In the algorithmic age, propaganda succeeds not by convincing, but by destabilising trust.* This is why authoritarian states find it so attractive: it is cheaper and more efficient to undermine adversaries' confidence in their institutions than to persuade them of the superiority of one's own.

Western democracies are particularly vulnerable to this new dynamic. Cold War propaganda was often easier to detect and counter, because it came with identifiable fingerprints: the accents of state broadcasters, the slogans of ideological pamphlets. Today's campaigns are distributed through networks of bots, influencers, and seemingly ordinary citizens. Moreover, the architecture of social media creates incentives for citizens themselves to participate in propagandistic dissemination. Outrage, fear, and indignation are not only emotional responses but also algorithmic currencies. A disinformation post gains reach not because a central authority orders it to, but because ordinary users share it, rewarded by the dopamine hit of engagement metrics. Thus, the line between victim and vector blurs. *Propaganda becomes participatory, crowdsourced through the very publics it manipulates.*

Drawing parallels with the Cold War also highlights the geopolitical competition at stake. Just as the United States and the Soviet Union once measured their influence through the number of countries aligned with their ideological blocs, today's digital powers compete over whose platforms, narratives, and algorithmic infrastructures dominate global information space. The export of platforms such as TikTok, Facebook, or YouTube is not simply a commercial story but a geopolitical one: whoever controls the dominant platforms controls the architecture through which virality operates. In Cold War terms, this is akin to controlling the radio frequencies and satellite networks through which propaganda once travelled—but with exponentially greater intimacy, as platforms now mediate the daily lives and relationships of billions.

Some argue that Propaganda 2.0 is not entirely novel, but simply a continuation of age-old psychological operations with new tools. Yet this underestimates the systemic differences. During the Cold War, propaganda relied on repetition, symbolism, and selective framing to shape attitudes over months or years. Today, virality can achieve in hours what once required years of cultural infiltration. Moreover, the use of algorithmic targeting allows campaigns to reach micro-audiences with tailored messages. A fabricated story need not convince the entire electorate; it can be directed at undecided voters in swing constituencies with uncanny precision. This is propaganda at the level of the individual, where each citizen inhabits a curated information environment optimised to exploit their particular fears or hopes. *It represents the granularisation of influence, a sharp departure from the blunt instruments of the past.*

The philosophical implications are profound. Cold War propaganda presupposed a contest between two versions of the world—capitalist democracy versus communist centralism. Propaganda 2.0, by contrast, thrives in the erosion of stable worldviews. It does not present a clear alternative but erodes the conditions under which alternatives can be meaningfully debated. This creates a paradox: while states weaponise virality for strategic ends, the long-term result may be a corrosion of all narrative authority, including their own. In this sense, authoritarian states play a dangerous game. By spreading disinformation abroad, they contribute to the global normalisation of distrust—a climate that can eventually seep back into their own information environments despite censorship. The Cold War may have ended with one system claiming victory, but Propaganda 2.0 offers no such resolution; its telos is not ideological triumph but epistemic exhaustion.

For democratic societies, the challenge lies in recognising that the new propaganda is not external to ordinary communication but woven into the architecture of everyday digital life. Efforts to counter it through fact-checking or media literacy, though valuable, often underestimate the structural force of virality. Just as Cold War states invested in counter-propaganda infrastructure—broadcasting their own messages, sponsoring cultural exchanges, and cultivating credibility—contemporary democracies must grapple with the need for systemic responses. This includes rethinking the design of platforms themselves, questioning whether algorithms optimised for engagement can coexist with the requirements of a functioning public sphere. *The battlefield of ideas has not disappeared; it has migrated into code.*

Propaganda 2.0 is not a simple continuation of the Cold War playbook, nor is it an entirely new phenomenon. It is a hybrid form—drawing on the objectives of the past while exploiting the unique affordances of algorithmic systems. The Cold War's propaganda wars were fought with broadcasts and slogans; today's with memes, hashtags, and viral videos. Yet the stakes remain eerily similar: control over how populations perceive reality, legitimacy, and power. What has changed is the tempo and topology of the contest. In a world where virality dictates visibility, propaganda is no longer a matter of broadcasting louder than one's rival. It is a matter of designing content that algorithms cannot resist amplifying, ensuring that it embeds itself within the daily rhythms of digital life. This shift marks the passage from propaganda as spectacle to propaganda as environment—a transformation as consequential for the twenty-first century as the Cold War's information wars were for the twentieth.

The Cost of Distrust

The strength of any society rests less on the raw accumulation of laws, weapons, or infrastructure than on something less tangible: trust. When citizens believe that the information they consume is broadly reliable, they can participate in collective decision-making, disagree constructively, and accept outcomes even when unfavourable. When that trust erodes, the very mechanics of governance falter. The paradox of the digital age is that humanity has never had so much access to information, yet rarely has it been so uncertain of its veracity. The result is a creeping corrosion of the social fabric, where every fact can be contested, every authority doubted, and every narrative dismissed as manipulation. *A society without trust in information does not simply debate less effectively—it begins to fracture at its core.*

Disinformation is not new; rumours have swayed wars, toppled leaders, and inflamed mobs for centuries. What is new is the algorithmic acceleration of these dynamics. Platforms designed to capture attention reward sensationalism and outrage, while filtering mechanisms create parallel realities for different groups. This produces an environment where two citizens of the same country may not simply disagree on policies, but fail to share even a basic set of facts. The American debate over COVID-19 vaccines illustrates the danger. Scientific evidence overwhelmingly demonstrated their effectiveness, yet disinformation campaigns—

some seeded by domestic actors, others by foreign adversaries—fuelled widespread scepticism. The consequence was not merely slower uptake of life-saving interventions, but an intensification of polarisation, with public health itself transformed into an ideological battleground. *When trust fractures, even matters of life and death become hostage to partisanship.*

The implications for governance are profound. Democracies function not because everyone agrees, but because enough citizens accept institutional legitimacy and factual baselines to enable compromise. If electoral results are consistently contested as illegitimate, the system cannot endure. The storming of the United States Capitol on 6 January 2021 stands as a vivid warning: when large segments of the population believe—without evidence—that an election was stolen, political disagreements no longer operate within the bounds of democratic procedure. They spill into outright confrontation. What should be a routine transfer of power becomes a crisis of sovereignty. Distrust transforms politics from a competition of policies into a contest over reality itself.

Authoritarian regimes face a different but related problem. While they may initially benefit from spreading disinformation abroad, at home they rely heavily on curated narratives to sustain legitimacy. Yet as deepfakes and digital manipulation proliferate, even citizens conditioned to accept official narratives may become sceptical. In Russia, where state television has long served as the central instrument of political control, younger generations exposed to digital platforms often treat both Kremlin narratives and Western reporting with suspicion, preferring instead to trust only their personal networks. On the surface this may look like resilience against manipulation, but it represents a deeper instability: *when trust in official information collapses, so does the capacity of governments—democratic or authoritarian—to mobilise collective action in crises.*

Distrust does not only undermine political processes; it corrodes social cohesion. In societies saturated with competing narratives, citizens retreat into identity-based enclaves where information is filtered by shared belief rather than by evidence. These echo chambers are comforting in their coherence, but they fragment the wider public sphere. Once fragmented, dialogue between groups becomes nearly impossible, for each is convinced the other is operating under falsehoods. The effects are visible in protests around climate change, migration, or policing, where both sides wield facts but reject each other's sources outright. *The battlefield shifts from policy differences to epistemic warfare: whose truth counts as truth?*

The economic consequences are equally striking. Trust is the lubricant of commerce as much as of governance. Financial markets rely on confidence in data, contracts, and regulatory oversight. If information integrity is compromised, investment falters and capital flows are distorted. Cryptocurrencies, often celebrated as instruments of decentralisation, exemplify this fragility. The sector thrives on narratives of transparency and liberation from state systems, yet it is rife with scams, manipulated markets, and disinformation-fuelled hype. Investors discover too late that the lack of trusted intermediaries magnifies vulnerability. Here, distrust does not merely paralyse governance—it destroys wealth and destabilises economies.

At the heart of the crisis lies a paradox. The very tools developed to democratise information—search engines, social platforms, recommendation systems—have undermined the collective trust necessary for democracy to function. Citizens are no longer passive recipients of centralised broadcasts; they are active participants in constructing, remixing, and disseminating narratives. This empowerment is double-edged. On one hand, it diversifies perspectives and breaks monopolies on truth. On the other, it renders consensus elusive. *When every citizen is their own broadcaster, society gains plurality but loses coherence.*

Philosophically, this raises a question long debated but newly urgent: what anchors shared reality? For centuries, authority rested in institutions—church, monarchy, press, academy—that could, however imperfectly, arbitrate truth claims. Their decline has coincided with the rise of distributed networks, where authority is crowd-sourced, unstable, and perpetually contested. Some celebrate this as liberation from gatekeepers, but the cost is mounting: without institutions trusted to adjudicate disputes over fact, societies become prone to manipulation, conspiracy, and paralysis. Trust, once eroded, is not easily rebuilt. History shows that it often takes catastrophes—wars, depressions, pandemics—to restore collective confidence in institutions. But waiting for catastrophe is a dangerous wager in a nuclear-armed, digitally interconnected world.

The cost of distrust is also measured in governance capacity. Effective governments rely on citizens who comply with rules not merely out of fear of punishment, but out of belief in legitimacy. Tax collection, public health campaigns, infrastructure development—all require cooperation rooted in trust. If every directive is met with suspicion, the state must rely on coercion, which is both expensive and unstable. The more citizens distrust government, the more authoritarian methods become tempting, creating a feedback loop where distrust breeds repression, and repression breeds further distrust. Democracies risk illiberal drift; authoritarian regimes risk brittle collapse. *The fracture of trust is the fracture of governance itself.*

Yet it would be too simple to suggest that trust can be restored by technological fixes alone. Fact-checking, algorithmic adjustments, and transparency measures are necessary but insufficient. Trust is not merely about the accuracy of information; it is about the perceived intentions of those who provide it. Citizens ask not only, "Is this true?" but also, "Why are you telling me this?" When institutions are seen as corrupt, self-serving, or captured by elites, even factual information will be dismissed. Rebuilding trust therefore requires addressing structural inequities and demonstrating that institutions serve the public good. Without this, any attempt to correct disinformation risks being perceived as just another manipulation.

The ultimate danger is not that people will believe falsehoods, but that they will believe nothing. A citizen who holds fast to a conspiracy theory can, in principle, still be debated, persuaded, or proven wrong. A citizen who believes that *all* sources are tainted, that *every* narrative is suspect, withdraws from the public sphere entirely. They cease to participate, to vote, to cooperate. This is the endpoint of distrust: not rage, but apathy. A society of apathetic citizens is ungovernable, for governance depends on engagement as much as obedience.

The cost of distrust, then, is not only measured in political crises or disinformation scandals. It is measured in the slow erosion of social glue, the hollowing out of collective capacity, and the transformation of politics into perpetual conflict over reality itself. Rebuilding trust will not be easy, but understanding the scale of what is at stake is the first step. *Without trust, societies do not merely argue; they unravel.*

Chapter 5

The Algorithmic State

Political power has always been mediated by technologies of governance. From the census tables of imperial China to the bureaucratic paperwork of modern nation-states, rulers have relied on information systems to know, classify, and manage their populations. What distinguishes the present moment is not merely the scale or speed of these systems, but their predictive capacity. States are no longer confined to registering what has happened; increasingly, they aspire to foresee what might occur, to pre-empt risks before they materialise, and to allocate resources based not on current need but on anticipated behaviour. *The state is becoming algorithmic, and in doing so it is redefining both its authority and its legitimacy.*

At the forefront of this shift lies predictive governance. Police departments deploy machine learning models to forecast where crimes are most likely to occur, adjusting patrol routes accordingly. Welfare agencies experiment with algorithms that estimate which claimants are most likely to commit fraud, directing scrutiny disproportionately toward the predicted few. Immigration authorities use automated risk scoring to determine which travellers warrant additional inspection or denial of entry. These tools are presented as rational, efficient, and impartial, promising to remove human bias and streamline scarce public resources. Yet they embed a profound transformation: the locus of state action moves from adjudicating present facts to policing future probabilities. For the citizen, this shift alters the very terms of belonging. No longer judged only by one's past deeds, one is increasingly evaluated by statistical projections of what one might do.

This raises uncomfortable questions about the bargain between efficiency and democratic oversight. The appeal of algorithmic governance is undeniable: fewer delays in bureaucratic processes, quicker responses to crises, and ostensibly objective decisions that spare citizens from the caprice of human officials. But what is surrendered in exchange? Oversight bodies often lack the expertise to interrogate opaque models, while citizens, confronted with decisions generated by black boxes, find their ability to challenge authority diminished. Efficiency becomes a justification for opacity, eroding the very accountability that democracy is meant to secure. *The danger is not only that efficiency will displace fairness, but that citizens may gradually acclimatise to this trade-off, normalising a governance model that is less contestable and more technocratic.*

The contrast between democratic and authoritarian applications of these technologies is often overstated. While China's social credit system is the most conspicuous example of algorithmic control—aggregating data from financial transactions, social media activity, and legal records to generate behavioural scores—it is less an aberration than a mirror held up to subtler Western practices. Credit scoring agencies in Europe and North America, risk-assessment tools in judicial sentencing, and the predictive flagging of welfare recipients all operate on similar logics, even if they lack the centralised spectacle of China's system. The difference is often one of degree, integration, and rhetoric rather than of kind. Citizens in liberal democracies may resist the label of "social credit", but their data is continuously harvested, scored, and acted upon in ways that shape their access to housing, employment, healthcare, and mobility. The convergence is disquieting: *states across ideological divides are discovering in algorithms a new mode of sovereignty, one that governs not only through law but through probability.*

Yet the promise of algorithmic governance is also shadowed by its fragility. As governments embed AI into critical systems—healthcare allocation, energy grids, cyber-defence—they risk becoming dependent on technologies they cannot fully understand or control. When these systems fail, the consequences are not abstract. In 2020, the Dutch government was forced to resign after a scandal involving an algorithm that falsely accused thousands of families of welfare fraud, many of them from minority backgrounds. Lives were upended, children removed from their parents, and trust in public institutions collapsed. In the United States, predictive policing tools have been shown to reinforce racial biases by disproportionately directing attention to communities already over-policed. These are not isolated mishaps; they reveal a structural fragility in delegating governance to systems whose logic remains hidden even to their designers. *The black box, once embraced as a neutral tool, becomes a potential site of governance breakdown.*

Philosophically, the rise of the algorithmic state raises questions about legitimacy that go beyond efficiency or error rates. The modern social contract rests on the premise that citizens are subjects of laws they can understand, contest, and ultimately change through political processes. When decision-making shifts to models that are inscrutable, dynamic, and often proprietary, that contract is weakened. How does one appeal a decision that no human has directly made? How does one deliberate about policies whose operational logic lies beyond public comprehension? Democratic institutions are predicated on transparency, yet algorithmic governance tends toward opacity. The result is not only a challenge to accountability but to the very possibility of democratic self-rule.

At the same time, it would be simplistic to frame the algorithmic state solely as a dystopian threat. Algorithms can, in principle, reduce corruption, counteract personal prejudice, and make scarce resources go further. They can detect fraud more effectively than overwhelmed human auditors, spot anomalies in cyber defences at speeds impossible for manual oversight, and coordinate emergency responses with unprecedented precision. For small states with limited bureaucratic capacity, these tools offer a way to deliver public goods that would otherwise remain out of reach. The real question is not whether algorithms should be used, but under what conditions, with what safeguards, and at what cost to the deeper values of democratic life.

This chapter examines these tensions: the allure of prediction, the temptation of efficiency, the convergence of surveillance practices across political systems, and the fragility introduced by opaque black-box models. It asks whether societies can harness algorithmic tools without eroding the very foundations of governance, and whether citizens will accept—or resist—the trade-offs implied by this transformation. For if the twentieth century was defined by the industrial state, governed through bureaucracies and mass institutions, the twenty-first may be defined by the algorithmic state, where sovereignty is exercised not just through laws and decrees but through datasets and models. *Understanding this shift is essential to understanding the future of political power itself.*

Governing by Prediction

The state has always sought to know its citizens, but never before has it aspired to anticipate them so completely. Prediction has become a new modality of governance: no longer content with reacting to what has happened, governments increasingly strive to manage populations by estimating what might occur. Artificial intelligence and algorithmic systems enable officials to identify likely offenders before crimes are committed, flag welfare recipients at higher risk of fraud before any misdeed takes place, and classify travellers as potential threats before they cross a border. This shift is not just technological; it is philosophical. It changes the relationship between citizen and state from one mediated by law and accountability to one shaped by probabilities and pre-emption.

The story of predictive policing illustrates this transformation vividly. Programmes like PredPol in the United States and equivalent tools in the United Kingdom were built on the assumption that crime, like weather, exhibits patterns that can be mapped and forecast. Historical data about burglaries, assaults, or thefts are fed into machine learning models that then generate "heat maps" of likely hotspots, directing police resources accordingly. Proponents argue this makes policing more efficient and evidence-based, allowing scarce patrols to be deployed where they are most needed. Yet critics have pointed out that the data used to train these systems is itself a record of past policing, not of all crime. Communities historically subject to heavy surveillance are thus flagged repeatedly as areas of heightened risk, creating feedback loops that entrench bias while presenting themselves as neutral outputs of an algorithm. The effect is not simply to predict crime but to reproduce inequalities under the guise of objectivity. *What appears as foresight can, in practice, be a reinforcement of historical prejudice, legitimised by mathematics.*

Welfare allocation offers another domain where prediction is transforming governance. Public assistance systems in the Netherlands, Australia, and the United States have experimented with algorithmic tools to identify fraud risk among claimants. On paper, the promise is clear: reduce waste, ensure fairness, and maintain public trust in the system by catching cheats before they exploit it. In practice, the consequences have often been devastating. The Dutch "Toeslagenaffaire", in which thousands of families—disproportionately from immigrant backgrounds—were falsely accused of benefit fraud by an automated risk-scoring system, led to bankruptcies, family separations, and the resignation of the government. Such cases reveal the fragility of prediction as a mode of welfare governance. Instead of ensuring efficient distribution, predictive models can erode trust in the very institutions they are meant to uphold, particularly when citizens cannot understand or contest the basis of the accusations against them. The drive for efficiency, when pursued without adequate safeguards, becomes indistinguishable from injustice.

Borders too are being reconfigured through prediction. Governments in North America and Europe increasingly use AI-driven risk assessment systems to decide which travellers merit closer inspection or exclusion.

Facial recognition technologies, passenger name record analysis, and behavioural profiling tools are deployed to generate risk scores in real time. The traveller becomes less an individual subject to law than a dataset to be evaluated. Here, prediction is not only about efficiency but about sovereignty itself. The ability to pre-emptively decide who may enter, who must be delayed, and who is turned away reflects the state's ultimate power to decide who belongs and who does not. But when such decisions are driven by opaque algorithms, often supplied by private vendors, accountability becomes elusive. A rejected traveller rarely learns what combination of variables marked them as a risk, nor do citizens know whether such systems reinforce existing prejudices against particular nationalities, religions, or socio-economic profiles. *Prediction, in this context, becomes a tool of exclusion without explanation, asserting authority while withholding transparency.*

The philosophical implications are far-reaching. Traditional governance rests on retrospective logic: crimes are punished after they occur, fraud is prosecuted after evidence emerges, and travellers are judged on the basis of actions or documents presented at the border. Predictive governance collapses this temporal sequence. It acts before wrongdoing occurs, or even before intent is established, on the basis of statistical probabilities. This raises a fundamental question: can a state legitimately sanction, restrict, or disadvantage individuals based not on what they have done but on what they might do? The predictive paradigm shifts the moral burden from proof to probability, from accountability to anticipation. *In doing so, it unsettles the principle that citizens are equal before the law, replacing it with a regime where they are stratified by risk scores and predictive markers.*

Proponents counter that prediction is simply a tool, one that can be used responsibly if designed with fairness, transparency, and oversight. They point out that prediction already governs many aspects of social life: insurance premiums, credit scores, and medical diagnoses all rely on probabilistic assessment. Why should governments not harness similar techniques to allocate resources more effectively, prevent harm, and protect the public? This argument is compelling, particularly in contexts where state capacity is stretched and efficiency gains can mean the difference between adequate service and collapse. But the analogy is imperfect. Insurance and credit scoring are market instruments; citizens can, at least in principle, choose different providers or opt out entirely. Governance, by contrast, is inescapable. When the state governs by prediction, it sets the rules of collective life in ways that individuals cannot avoid, challenge, or exit. The stakes are higher, and the safeguards must therefore be stronger.

Moreover, predictive systems are not static. Machine learning models evolve as they are trained on new data, meaning the criteria by which citizens are judged can shift without public awareness. A welfare claimant deemed low risk today may be flagged tomorrow due to changes in the model's weighting of variables, yet the claimant may never know why. This dynamism makes governance by prediction profoundly different from governance by law. Laws can be read, debated, and contested; predictive models cannot be so easily scrutinised. The opacity of algorithms, whether due to their technical complexity or proprietary protection, introduces a new layer of unaccountability. *The state's authority is thus refracted through systems that are neither transparent nor stable, eroding the citizen's ability to understand or contest the rules by which they are governed.*

The convergence of predictive tools across policing, welfare, and border control underscores their broader political function: to manage uncertainty in populations. Crime, fraud, and migration are all phenomena perceived by states as sources of disorder. Prediction offers a way to pre-empt disorder, to render populations legible not only as they are but as they might become. This ambition is as old as statecraft itself, yet its current manifestation carries new risks. By privileging probability over personhood, predictive governance risks transforming citizens into perpetual suspects, never fully free from the statistical shadows cast by their data.

Ultimately, governing by prediction is not just a technical adjustment; it represents a reconfiguration of sovereignty. It shifts the balance between citizen and state, recasting rights and obligations in probabilistic terms. It offers efficiency and control but at the cost of transparency, accountability, and equality. Whether societies accept this trade depends not only on the performance of predictive systems but on the values they are willing to uphold. Prediction, after all, is not destiny. It is a choice about how power is exercised, and about what kind of relationship governments wish to forge with those they govern.

Efficiency vs. Legitimacy

Few dilemmas of the digital age cut as sharply as the trade-off between efficiency and legitimacy in governance. On one side lies the promise of algorithmic systems: streamlined bureaucracy, instantaneous decision-making, optimised allocation of resources. On the other stands the slow, deliberative machinery of democratic oversight, with its checks, balances, debates, and compromises. The question is whether citizens, weary of institutional gridlock and inefficiency, will accept governance by algorithm, and if so, what democratic values are sacrificed in the process. The real issue is not whether efficiency is desirable—it obviously is—but whether a state that privileges efficiency over legitimacy risks hollowing out the very foundation of political authority.

The attraction of efficiency is undeniable, particularly in contexts where democratic institutions appear paralysed. Public frustration at legislative stalemates, bureaucratic red tape, and policy delays has created fertile ground for the idea that algorithms might govern more effectively than politicians. Estonia is often celebrated as a model of the "digital state," where e-governance platforms handle everything from voting to tax filing with minimal friction. In such systems, decisions can be executed with a speed and precision impossible for traditional bureaucracies. The citizen experience improves, trust in government services appears to rise, and states present themselves as technologically progressive. Yet efficiency is not the same as legitimacy. A tax refund issued promptly by an algorithm may inspire satisfaction, but decisions involving policing, welfare, or immigration require more than procedural speed: they require justification that citizens find morally and politically acceptable. *A decision delivered in milliseconds is not inherently a decision that can command consent.*

The trade-off becomes clearer when algorithms are used to replace, rather than assist, democratic processes. Consider predictive policing systems deployed in American and European cities. These tools promise efficiency: fewer patrol hours wasted, more targeted interventions, reduced crime. But they short-circuit democratic deliberation about what policing should prioritise, which communities should be protected, and what level of surveillance is acceptable. Citizens never debated whether statistical risk models should define policing strategies; such tools were often introduced quietly, through procurement contracts and technical trials. The result is governance without the visible process of governance. Efficiency here does not supplement legitimacy but sidesteps it, raising the question of whether citizens are governed by laws they have consented to or by algorithms they cannot see.

The welfare state offers another revealing case. When Denmark, the United Kingdom, and Australia deployed algorithmic systems to detect fraud among benefit recipients, the intention was straightforward: make distribution more efficient and ensure public money was not wasted. Yet the consequences revealed the fragility of legitimacy when efficiency alone drives decision-making. Many individuals were falsely flagged, burdened with debt or denied benefits without clear recourse. Citizens were not only harmed materially but also alienated from their governments. They no longer trusted that the system treated them fairly. The legitimacy of welfare institutions depends not merely on delivering benefits quickly but on embodying the principle of justice. An efficient system that undermines this principle erodes its own authority, no matter how optimised its processes appear on paper.

Efficiency also creates a subtle cultural shift in governance: it recasts citizens as clients or users of state services rather than as participants in political life. Algorithms deliver services rapidly and impersonally, bypassing human discretion, which many see as a virtue. But in stripping away the slow negotiations, the explanations, and the possibility of appeal, states risk treating citizens as problems to be processed rather than agents with voice and dignity. Democratic legitimacy requires that people see themselves not merely as recipients of government outputs but as co-authors of collective rules. *Efficiency that neglects participation risks transforming governance from a political enterprise into a technocratic service industry.*

Of course, efficiency and legitimacy need not always conflict. There are domains where the two align, particularly when transparency and accountability are built into algorithmic systems. Singapore's use of data-driven dashboards to monitor transport networks, for example, has improved efficiency while also enhancing legitimacy, since citizens can see in real time how policies reduce congestion and improve services. But this alignment depends on careful design and, crucially, on the scope of decisions delegated to machines. When algorithms handle technical optimisation tasks—traffic flows, hospital scheduling—the legitimacy costs are minimal. When they make decisions that touch directly on justice, liberty, or inclusion, efficiency gains can quickly turn into legitimacy deficits.

The deeper philosophical issue is that legitimacy requires slowness. Democratic oversight is intentionally inefficient because it must reconcile competing values, accommodate dissent, and provide space for accountability. Parliamentary debates, public consultations, judicial reviews—these are not inefficiencies in the trivial sense but essential practices that transform state power into legitimate authority. To trade these for efficiency is to misunderstand their function. An algorithm may calculate the fastest route to a policy outcome, but it cannot replace the deliberative process through which societies decide which outcomes are acceptable in the first place. *Efficiency can deliver means, but legitimacy must determine ends.*

Yet citizens are not always patient. Faced with crises—economic recessions, pandemics, climate shocks—the appeal of efficiency intensifies. During the COVID-19 pandemic, governments worldwide turned to algorithmic tools to allocate vaccines, track infections, and enforce lockdowns. Many citizens accepted these measures, valuing rapid response over deliberative process. The crisis revealed how easily exceptional circumstances can normalise governance by algorithm. What begins as a temporary efficiency measure can become a permanent fixture, shifting the balance between oversight and optimisation in ways that citizens never explicitly endorsed. Crises thus act as accelerators, testing whether societies will safeguard legitimacy even under pressure, or whether they will cede it in pursuit of immediate efficiency.

The long-term costs of privileging efficiency are not always visible in the short term. A state that governs efficiently through opaque algorithms may appear stable until trust suddenly collapses. Legitimacy erodes quietly, as citizens cease to believe that decisions are made in their name or for reasons they can recognise. The Dutch childcare benefits scandal, in which thousands of families were unjustly accused of fraud by an algorithmic system, demonstrates how such erosion can explode into political crisis. What was framed as a technical fix to improve efficiency ultimately delegitimised an entire government. *Efficiency gains are fragile if legitimacy is not sustained alongside them.*

The critical question, then, is whether societies can craft governance models that integrate efficiency without undermining legitimacy. This requires recognising that legitimacy is not a secondary concern but the foundation upon which all efficiency rests. Transparent systems, meaningful oversight, and avenues for contestation are not inefficiencies to be eliminated but safeguards that preserve the political fabric. Democracies that neglect this lesson may find that they gain speed at the cost of direction, achieving more in the short term while corroding their authority in the long term.

Citizens will indeed make trade-offs, but the terms of those trade-offs matter. When people consent to algorithmic tools in service of clear, transparent, and accountable goals, efficiency can coexist with legitimacy. When tools are imposed silently, without debate or recourse, efficiency becomes an authoritarian temptation—seductive in its promise of order but corrosive in its erosion of trust. The balance between efficiency and legitimacy is thus not a technical problem but a political choice, one that defines what it means to be governed in an age of algorithms.

Surveillance Sovereignty

The most striking feature of modern state power is not its brute force but its capacity to watch, record, and anticipate. If the twentieth century was defined by ideological competition between capitalism and communism, the twenty-first may be shaped by a quieter struggle: the extent to which states claim sovereignty through surveillance. China's social credit system has become a global symbol of algorithmic control, a vast infrastructure of monitoring that blends financial data, social behaviour, and political loyalty into a single index of trustworthiness. It is often depicted in the West as a dystopian aberration, an authoritarian experiment with little in common with liberal democracies. Yet the distance between Beijing's project and Western forms of digital governance is narrower than many assume. While the Chinese state pursues overt behavioural scoring, Western governments increasingly rely on fragmented but converging mechanisms of surveillance that, in practice, achieve similar effects. What emerges is a global architecture in which *sovereignty is reasserted through visibility*—citizens' lives rendered transparent to the state, not as a matter of open deliberation but as a condition of participation in modern society.

The Chinese system deserves careful attention not because it is unique but because it reveals the logic of surveillance sovereignty in its clearest form. Announced in 2014 and framed as a project to build trust in markets and society, the social credit system operates as a hybrid of state and private data-gathering. It collates information from financial records, criminal histories, online behaviour, and even everyday infractions such as jaywalking or unpaid bills. Rewards are offered to those with high scores—easier access to loans, faster visa approvals—while penalties fall on the untrustworthy, from travel restrictions to public naming-and-shaming. The striking feature is not just the breadth of surveillance but its moral claim: that good citizenship can be objectively measured and enforced through data. This reframes governance as behavioural engineering, with the state positioned as the arbiter of trust. What makes the system so potent is its integration—different streams of information coalesce into a unified infrastructure of control.

Western observers often recoil at the system, yet their own societies are increasingly stitched together by forms of algorithmic monitoring that differ in degree but not in principle. Credit scores in the United States, developed originally to standardise lending decisions, now influence employment prospects, housing opportunities, and even insurance rates. Policing in the United Kingdom and United States has embraced predictive algorithms that score neighbourhoods or individuals on their likelihood of committing crime. Border agencies across Europe deploy risk-assessment tools that categorise travellers and asylum seekers into bands of trustworthiness. Each system may lack the totalising ambition of China's model, but the underlying mechanism is similar: individual behaviour is captured, quantified, and fed back into governance as a tool of control. *The social credit system is shocking to Western sensibilities not because the logic is alien, but because it is made explicit.*

The deeper convergence lies in how states justify surveillance. Both authoritarian and democratic governments frame it as necessary for security, efficiency, or trust. Chinese officials argue that social credit fosters responsibility and harmony in a society lacking institutional trust. Western governments claim that algorithmic surveillance enhances fairness, reduces human bias, and makes bureaucracies more responsive. In both cases, legitimacy is sought through an appeal to rationality: surveillance is presented not as an encroachment but as an optimisation of governance. Citizens are told that systems are neutral, objective, and in their collective interest. What differs is the political framing. In China, the narrative is one of moral improvement under state guidance; in the West, it is one of consumer choice and administrative efficiency. Yet both rationales converge on the same outcome: citizens increasingly live in environments where data trails dictate opportunities and constraints.

The surveillance state is not built solely through government fiat; private companies act as indispensable partners. In China, platforms such as Alibaba and Tencent provide financial and behavioural data that feed state systems, effectively merging commercial and political oversight. In the West, social media firms, credit agencies, and data brokers accumulate vast stores of information that governments tap for policing, immigration control, or intelligence. The Snowden revelations underscored the porous boundary between corporate and state surveillance in liberal democracies. The distinction between state and market control—often cited as a bulwark of Western freedom—dissolves when both rely on the same infrastructures of data extraction. The central issue is not whether surveillance originates in Beijing or Silicon Valley, but how much autonomy citizens retain when their lives are legible only through the metrics others impose.

What makes surveillance sovereignty distinct from past forms of state power is its preventative character. Traditional sovereignty often revealed itself through punishment after transgression; surveillance sovereignty seeks to pre-empt undesirable behaviour altogether. The Chinese state uses facial recognition at train stations not simply to catch fare dodgers but to deter them by ensuring the certainty of detection. Western welfare agencies employ fraud-detection algorithms to prevent claims from being processed in the first place. Border systems assign risk scores to travellers before they set foot in a country. The shift is subtle but profound: *citizens no longer encounter the state primarily when they break the law, but when their predicted risk profile triggers intervention.* Sovereignty becomes less about enforcing law retrospectively and more about shaping the field of possibility in advance.

Critics often emphasise the authoritarian potential of such systems, and rightly so, yet it is important to acknowledge their democratic allure. Surveillance sovereignty is sold to citizens as protection against disorder, inefficiency, or unfairness. Predictive policing is defended as a way to reduce crime in vulnerable neighbourhoods; credit scoring is framed as a means of granting fairer access to loans by using data rather than personal prejudice; airport security algorithms promise to speed travellers through checkpoints while targeting only high-risk passengers. These systems thrive not only because states impose them but because citizens, at least initially, find them convenient, efficient, or even just. The danger is that this convenience masks the political stakes: the subtle reconfiguration of what it means to be free, equal, and accountable under conditions of total visibility.

The global convergence around surveillance sovereignty raises a paradox. States compete fiercely in geopolitics, yet they increasingly adopt similar infrastructures of control. China exports its surveillance technologies to countries in Africa and the Middle East, embedding its model abroad. Meanwhile, Western firms dominate global data markets, ensuring that their systems too become standards across jurisdictions. What emerges is not a clash of civilisations but a fusion of techniques: *a shared grammar of surveillance that transcends political systems.* The language differs—social harmony in China, consumer efficiency in the West—but the grammar is the same: govern by watching, score by prediction, enforce by data.

This convergence invites a rethinking of sovereignty itself. In the classical sense, sovereignty was about territory, borders, and the monopoly on legitimate violence. In the algorithmic age, sovereignty is increasingly about information: the ability to see, process, and intervene in the lives of citizens through their digital traces. States that fail to master this capacity risk appearing weak, unable to maintain order or allocate resources effectively. Surveillance becomes not only a tool of internal control but a marker of geopolitical strength. To govern without visibility is to cede sovereignty; to govern with visibility is to risk legitimacy. The tension is one that every society must confront, whether under the banner of democracy or authoritarianism.

Surveillance sovereignty thus stands as one of the defining features of our century. China's social credit system may be the most visible expression, but it is not the exception—it is a mirror. Western societies may recoil at its bluntness, but their own fragmented systems, layered across finance, policing, welfare, and borders, amount to a mosaic that increasingly resembles the same logic. The danger is not that the West will become China, but that in chasing efficiency, security, and optimisation, it will arrive at similar forms of control without ever admitting the choice. The sovereignty of the future will not be asserted with flags or armies alone but through the infrastructures of visibility that render populations transparent. The question is whether societies will recognise the cost of that transparency before the bargain is complete.

The Fragility of Black Boxes

The very systems entrusted with safeguarding lives, securing nations, and managing scarce resources are increasingly ones we do not fully understand. Artificial intelligence has been celebrated as a tool of precision, efficiency, and speed, yet its most advanced forms often operate as opaque entities—black boxes whose inner logic is indecipherable even to their designers. The paradox is stark: as societies hand over critical governance functions to these models, their opacity introduces vulnerabilities that are rarely acknowledged until failure strikes. The fragility of black-box governance is not a speculative problem but a present and growing reality, one that becomes most dangerous when decisions are high stakes and errors, however rare, cascade into crises.

Healthcare offers one of the clearest illustrations of this tension. Hospitals around the world have adopted machine-learning systems to triage patients, allocate scarce resources, and predict medical outcomes. In the United States, a widely used risk prediction algorithm was found to systematically underestimate the healthcare needs of Black patients because it used past healthcare spending as a proxy for need. Since Black patients historically had less access to medical services, the algorithm concluded they were healthier than they actually were. Millions of patients were quietly disadvantaged, not through overt discrimination but through the model's hidden assumptions. This case exemplifies the fragility of opaque systems: when they fail, they fail silently, embedding bias and error deep within the machinery of governance. The failure is not technical alone but institutional—policymakers and administrators often treat the algorithm's outputs as authoritative, without the tools to interrogate how those outputs are produced.

The stakes are even higher when black-box systems govern security. Cyber-defence increasingly relies on AI to detect anomalies in vast streams of network traffic, flagging potential intrusions before they can escalate. Yet adversarial attacks—where malicious actors subtly manipulate input data—can render even the most sophisticated detection models useless. A system that can be deceived by a carefully crafted pattern of packets may allow catastrophic breaches to pass unnoticed. The opacity of the model means defenders cannot easily discern why it classifies some anomalies as harmless and others as threats. In such domains, *a failure to explain is a failure to govern.* Without transparency, the chain of accountability snaps, leaving states vulnerable to errors they cannot trace or correct.

Black-box fragility extends to border control, welfare distribution, and criminal justice. In the United Kingdom, the Home Office used a secretive algorithm to flag visa applications for potential risk, effectively creating a fast lane and a slow lane for migrants. When challenged in court, the department could not fully explain the criteria by which applications were scored. In welfare systems, fraud-detection models routinely block benefits based on opaque risk assessments, leaving vulnerable citizens with little recourse. In predictive policing, opaque algorithms have been shown to reinforce patterns of over-policing in marginalised communities, embedding social biases into supposedly objective systems. What unites these cases is the abdication of visibility: citizens are subject to decisions that shape their lives, yet neither they nor their governments can meaningfully interrogate the logic behind those decisions.

Supporters of black-box models often argue that accuracy should outweigh interpretability. Deep learning systems, they contend, are simply too complex to yield to human explanation; what matters is that they work. This argument carries weight when predictive accuracy truly saves lives—as in certain applications of medical imaging, where models detect tumours invisible to the human eye. Yet governance is not reducible to accuracy alone. A healthcare system that cannot explain why one patient receives treatment while another does not may erode trust even if outcomes are statistically improved. A cyber-defence system that fails without warning undermines not just technical security but institutional legitimacy. Governance demands accountability, and accountability cannot be outsourced to inscrutable machines.

There is also a strategic dimension to fragility. States that rely on black-box systems for critical infrastructure expose themselves to adversaries who may exploit their opacity. If decision-making cannot be traced, errors cannot be corrected quickly; if models cannot be interrogated, backdoors may remain undetected. This creates a peculiar vulnerability: societies may appear resilient because their systems function smoothly, but when failures do occur, they are sudden, opaque, and difficult to recover from. Fragility, in this sense, is not about the frequency of failure but the inability to withstand it. A transparent but imperfect system can adapt; a black box may collapse under the weight of its own secrecy.

The appeal of black boxes is undeniable. They promise efficiency where bureaucracies are slow, consistency where human judgement is biased, and foresight where traditional governance is reactive. Their outputs arrive in neat probabilities and rankings that suggest objectivity. Policymakers, under pressure to deliver results, may prefer these tools precisely because they obscure complexity: they provide the comfort of certainty without the burden of justification. Yet *the very features that make black boxes attractive—speed, complexity, opacity—are those that render them brittle when embedded in governance.* What is gained in efficiency may be lost in legitimacy, and what is gained in predictive power may be lost in resilience.

Some argue that fragility can be mitigated through explainable AI, an emerging field that seeks to render models interpretable without sacrificing performance. Techniques such as feature attribution, model simplification, or surrogate modelling provide partial windows into otherwise opaque systems. Yet these solutions are imperfect, often offering approximations rather than genuine explanations. Moreover, the politics of explanation cannot be ignored: an explanation that satisfies engineers may not satisfy policymakers, and one that satisfies policymakers may not satisfy citizens. The fragility of black boxes is not simply technical but democratic. It lies in the gap between what systems can explain and what societies require to grant consent.

Philosophically, the reliance on opaque systems raises an old but urgent question: can authority be legitimate if it cannot be understood? Traditional political theory has long wrestled with the tension between expertise and consent. Citizens routinely defer to doctors, engineers, and economists whose knowledge exceeds their own. Yet this deference is grounded in institutions of trust and accountability. A patient may not understand the molecular mechanisms of a drug, but they trust the regulatory framework that ensures its safety. Black-box governance disrupts this balance. It demands trust without comprehension, obedience without scrutiny. Such trust is brittle, for when failures surface—as they inevitably do—they provoke not just criticism of the system but disillusionment with the institutions that adopted it.

The fragility of black boxes is thus not an abstract problem of technology but a practical challenge of governance. Healthcare systems, cyber-defence operations, welfare agencies, and border controls cannot afford brittle foundations. Opaque models may offer short-term efficiency, but in the long run they risk undermining the very legitimacy on which effective governance depends. The central question is not whether societies will use AI in governance—they already do—but how they will confront the trade-off between opacity and accountability. To ignore the fragility of black boxes is to invite breakdowns that are as sudden as they are irreparable. The task ahead is not to retreat from AI but to demand systems that can be interrogated, contested, and understood, even at the cost of some efficiency. For in governance, unlike in pure prediction, *explanation is not a luxury—it is the condition of resilience.*

Chapter 6

The Corporate Empires

The modern state has long been defined by its monopoly over the levers of coercion, the ability to set rules and enforce them, and the privilege of shaping the economic and security order in which citizens live. Yet as artificial intelligence becomes the central infrastructure of twenty-first-century life, these functions are no longer the sole preserve of governments. A new form of authority has emerged, operating through boardrooms rather than parliaments, shareholder meetings rather than electoral assemblies, and contracts rather than treaties. The great technology corporations—Google, Microsoft, Amazon, Meta, OpenAI and their peers—have built digital empires that do not merely provide services but increasingly define the conditions under which states themselves can act. Their reach is not territorial but infrastructural, embedded in cloud servers, proprietary algorithms, data monopolies, and software ecosystems. The challenge for the twenty-first century is that these corporate powers are not secondary actors in global politics. They are fast becoming shadow states, whose decisions rival and sometimes surpass those of elected governments.

The analogy of a shadow state is not rhetorical flourish. Consider the way Google's search algorithms effectively determine what constitutes authoritative knowledge for billions of people each day. Governments may set curricula, regulate textbooks, and fund public education, but when citizens want to know the answer to a question—from medical symptoms to political candidates—it is Google's opaque ranking system that decides what information they encounter first. Microsoft, through its Azure cloud, provides the computational backbone not only for private enterprise but also for government operations, from military contracts with the US Department of Defense to health data storage agreements with European states. OpenAI, though far smaller in staff and budget than a nation-state, has found its models integrated into foreign policy briefings, corporate strategy, and law enforcement applications. These corporations establish de facto standards of knowledge, security, and interaction without waiting for the slow machinery of democratic oversight to catch up. Their influence arises not from lobbying alone but from indispensability: governments themselves have become clients.

This dependence has unsettling implications. If the classic hallmark of sovereignty is autonomy in decision-making, then states that cannot function without access to private digital infrastructure risk ceding part of their sovereignty to corporate boards. The migration of military, health, and justice systems to cloud platforms exemplifies this bargain. A state may fund its own armies and courts, but if its data processing and cyber-defence capacities are rented from Amazon Web Services or Microsoft, the locus of authority becomes blurred. Who truly governs when the operational backbone of a nation depends on systems owned, updated, and secured by profit-driven firms headquartered abroad? This is no longer a speculative question. Estonia's pioneering e-government system relies heavily on cloud and blockchain infrastructures developed in partnership with private entities. During cyber-attacks in 2007, Estonia's reliance on foreign-based data centres revealed both the strengths and vulnerabilities of such arrangements.

The corporate role extends beyond passive service provision. In security and defence, partnerships between governments and private firms are constructing what might be described as *private militaries of code*. Palantir, a company that emerged from Silicon Valley but now operates at the heart of intelligence analysis for Western governments, exemplifies this role. Its software shapes counterterrorism strategies, battlefield decisions, and surveillance policies, giving a single company extraordinary leverage over the conduct of war and security. In autonomous weapons development, private firms contribute algorithms that can distinguish targets, pilot drones, and even recommend lethal decisions. States that rely on such systems are effectively delegating sovereign acts of war to proprietary code. The boundary between public authority and private enterprise blurs further when companies sell these systems internationally, making them actors in global arms markets traditionally controlled by state policy.

This dynamic is not confined to the battlefield. Corporate AI systems increasingly mediate international negotiations, trade, and diplomacy. When the European Union attempted to regulate AI through its sweeping AI Act, it found itself in constant consultation with the very corporations it sought to regulate. Draft provisions were softened or delayed after lobbying efforts highlighted the risk of stifling innovation or driving companies offshore. The result was a policy environment in which corporate priorities shaped the pace and content of international governance. Similarly, when developing nations negotiate access to cloud services, data storage, or AI tools, they often face contractual terms dictated by corporations rather than bilateral agreements between states. Diplomacy becomes not only state-to-state but state-to-corporation, with private firms acting as gatekeepers to essential technologies.

The cost of this dependence is not always visible in immediate crises but manifests in the slow reconfiguration of power. When governments shape health policies around data analytics supplied by private companies, or when foreign ministries design strategy with the aid of corporate AI models, sovereignty becomes tethered to systems over which citizens exercise little oversight. The locus of accountability shifts. Elected officials can be voted out of office, but shareholders cannot be removed by a general election. Nations risk being governed in practice by invisible terms of service written in Silicon Valley legal departments rather than by laws debated in parliamentary chambers. *The very idea of democratic consent is strained when the essential conditions of governance are set by entities that owe no duty to the electorate.*

Defenders of corporate influence argue that firms deliver efficiencies governments cannot. Technology companies innovate faster, attract top talent, and operate without the bureaucratic drag of public institutions. In domains like cybersecurity or generative AI, where states struggle to recruit sufficient expertise, partnerships with the private sector may appear not only pragmatic but essential. Yet this pragmatism creates dependency loops. The more a government outsources, the less capacity it retains, and the less capacity it retains, the more it must outsource. Over time, sovereignty becomes a managed service, rented at scale from multinational firms whose first loyalty is to shareholders, not citizens. This dynamic is particularly visible in developing countries, where governments adopt turnkey AI solutions offered by corporations to manage policing, healthcare, or taxation. These states acquire not only software but entire governance architectures designed abroad, locking them into dependencies that are difficult to escape.

Corporate empires also shape geopolitics indirectly, by controlling the flows of data and computational power that undergird modern economies. Consider how export controls imposed by the United States on advanced chips manufactured by Nvidia have been wielded as instruments of foreign policy. Although the decision is governmental, the leverage derives from corporate monopoly over cutting-edge hardware. Similarly, debates over

TikTok's ownership and data flows illustrate how a single platform can become a flashpoint in international relations, prompting threats of bans, divestments, and retaliations. These cases reveal a new form of diplomacy where corporate assets themselves become geopolitical bargaining chips. States cannot ignore the corporations because the corporations themselves are integral components of global infrastructure.

One might ask whether this corporate ascendancy represents a temporary imbalance or a structural shift in world politics. Historical parallels suggest the latter. The British East India Company once operated as both a corporation and a colonial government, with its own armies, tax systems, and treaties. Its collapse was precipitated not by inefficiency but by the intolerable political consequences of a private entity wielding state-like powers. Today's technology giants are not colonial companies in the same mould, but they share a crucial feature: the ability to dictate terms of governance across borders without direct democratic accountability. Unlike the East India Company, however, their authority is not territorial but infrastructural. They govern through code, data, and networks, extending power into every society that relies on their systems.

The theme of this chapter is not corporate villainy but structural reality. Corporations have become indispensable because they control the core resources of the AI age: data, computation, and expertise. Governments cannot easily replicate these capacities. Yet indispensability should not be mistaken for legitimacy. The danger is that societies sleepwalk into an arrangement where private empires wield sovereign authority by default rather than design. The task is to recognise this shift, to examine its consequences for sovereignty, legitimacy, and democracy, and to consider how governance can be reclaimed or rebalanced in a world where corporations hold levers once reserved for states.

This chapter will trace how these dynamics manifest across different domains. It will consider corporations as shadow states that set the practical terms of AI access and use. It will explore how private firms develop cyber and military capabilities that rival or exceed those of governments, functioning as private militaries of code. It will analyse the ways in which nations outsource policy-making to platforms, becoming dependent on shareholder-driven interests, and it will show how corporate AI systems increasingly dictate the course of international diplomacy and trade. Together, these themes reveal the contours of a new global order where the question is not whether corporations will influence governance but how far their empire-building will be allowed to proceed. To understand this transformation is to confront one of the central political questions of the AI century: who governs when the code that runs society belongs to private hands?

Tech Giants as Shadow States

The authority of the modern state was once inseparable from its monopoly over law, currency, and force. Yet in the twenty-first century, another kind of authority has emerged, one not vested in constitutions or armies but in server farms, code repositories, and proprietary datasets. Corporations such as Google, Microsoft, and OpenAI have come to rival—and in certain respects, surpass—nation-states in setting the terms of access to artificial intelligence. These firms are not merely market leaders; they act as *sovereign architects* of the digital environment, determining what tools citizens, companies, and governments may use, under what conditions, and with what limits. The most striking feature of this transformation is that it has occurred quietly, often framed as the natural progress of innovation rather than a radical shift in political power.

To grasp the scale of this development, one must first consider the infrastructure upon which AI rests. Large-scale computing requires vast data centres, expensive chips, proprietary training datasets, and highly specialised expertise. Only a handful of corporations command these resources at global scale. Google's control of search and advertising has created unparalleled access to behavioural data, which in turn fuels its AI development. Microsoft, through its cloud platform Azure, holds contracts with governments and militaries worldwide, making its infrastructure a *strategic dependency* for states themselves. OpenAI, though younger and smaller, has positioned itself as a gatekeeper of advanced generative models, offering controlled access via API rather than wholesale distribution. In each case, the ability to *decide who may use cutting-edge AI, how, and for what purposes* rests not with parliaments or ministries but with private boards and corporate policies.

The question of control is not abstract but visible in everyday practice. When OpenAI decided against open-sourcing its most powerful language models, citing risks of misuse, it was in effect making a decision of the kind states traditionally reserve for themselves: balancing security against liberty. Similarly, when Google introduced restrictions on political advertising through its platforms, it directly shaped the contours of democratic debate in multiple countries, without a vote or public deliberation. Microsoft's partnership with the Pentagon to provide augmented-reality headsets for soldiers illustrates the fusion of corporate capacity with state military power, yet the underlying intellectual property remains under corporate ownership. These examples demonstrate that *the levers of governance have begun to migrate out of government hands and into private ones.*

The comparison to states becomes sharper when one examines the tools of enforcement. Traditional governments wield the threat of sanctions, imprisonment, or military force to uphold their authority. Technology firms, lacking territorial power, enforce compliance through access and exclusion. A developer who violates platform policies may be barred from using APIs, effectively exiled from the digital economy. Entire companies may find their business models destroyed overnight by a change in algorithmic ranking, as has been the fate of countless small publishers and retailers dependent on Google search or Facebook traffic. This kind of power does not rely on coercion in the conventional sense; it rests on indispensability. *When a system becomes the gateway to markets, knowledge, or communication, control of that system becomes a form of sovereignty.*

Critics might argue that corporate power, however vast, is constrained by regulation. Yet regulatory frameworks lag far behind technological change. Governments attempting to impose AI rules often find themselves negotiating not with an industry at large but with a small handful of firms whose expertise and infrastructure they cannot do without. The European Union's AI Act, touted as the world's first comprehensive AI regulation, has already been watered down under pressure from corporate lobbying, with significant exemptions granted to foundation models. Meanwhile, the United States has largely deferred to voluntary safety commitments negotiated directly with companies, effectively outsourcing governance to the very entities it claims to regulate. In both cases, public institutions appear less as sovereign arbiters than as negotiating partners, compelled to balance the demands of innovation with the risks of dependency.

The concentration of AI capacity also raises the problem of geopolitical asymmetry. Smaller nations face a stark choice: either align themselves with the technological standards of American firms or risk exclusion from the most advanced tools altogether. This dependence mirrors earlier moments in history when access to nuclear technology or financial networks shaped international hierarchies. Yet AI differs in that it permeates every layer of society—education, healthcare, security, commerce—such that exclusion is not merely a disadvantage but a form of marginalisation. For many developing countries, the terms of AI access will be set not through treaties or multilateral organisations but through corporate licensing agreements.

This is diplomacy by contract rather than by council, with private firms dictating the practical contours of sovereignty.

The ethical implications of this corporate sovereignty are profound. States, at least in principle, are accountable to their citizens through elections, constitutions, and legal checks. Corporations, by contrast, are accountable to shareholders and markets. When OpenAI decides to restrict model access in the name of "safety," whose safety is being prioritised? When Microsoft negotiates contracts with defence ministries, are the interests of global peace weighed against the imperative of shareholder return? When Google adjusts search algorithms, what epistemic values—accuracy, engagement, profit—are being optimised? *The absence of democratic accountability means that decisions of immense societal consequence are made behind closed doors, by actors with no direct responsibility to the public.*

Yet it would be too simple to frame these corporations as usurpers of state power. They have become indispensable precisely because states themselves are incapable of matching their technical capacity. Governments that lack the resources to build their own large language models or to maintain massive cloud infrastructures inevitably turn to the private sector. The United States government relies on Amazon and Microsoft for secure cloud hosting of classified data. The United Kingdom has turned to Palantir to manage NHS data analytics, despite public unease. These are not isolated choices but systemic dependencies. In this sense, corporate ascendancy is less an act of conquest than a reflection of governmental incapacity. *The state has outsourced not just its tools but parts of its sovereignty.*

The deeper question is whether this arrangement is sustainable. If corporations continue to expand their control over the infrastructures of knowledge, security, and communication, they may become not merely partners of states but their effective superiors. The logic of shareholder value will dictate not only product design but also the conditions under which societies access core technologies. States may attempt to reclaim authority through regulation or nationalisation, but such moves require political will and technical competence that many governments currently lack. Others may attempt to build their own alternatives, as China has done with Baidu and Huawei, yet this approach often produces national walled gardens rather than global commons. In either case, the reality remains: *the commanding heights of AI are controlled by a handful of corporations whose reach transcends borders, jurisdictions, and electoral cycles.*

The emergence of tech giants as shadow states marks a reconfiguration of political order. It challenges the assumption that sovereignty resides only in governments and that corporations are mere economic actors. It forces societies to confront uncomfortable questions about legitimacy, accountability, and control. If governance is defined by the ability to set rules, allocate resources, and shape collective futures, then Google, Microsoft, and OpenAI are already governing in meaningful ways. They are drafting the constitutions of the digital age—not in parliaments or congresses but in code and licensing agreements. Whether states reclaim authority or accept subordination will shape the trajectory of democracy itself in the age of artificial intelligence.

Private Militaries of Code

The privatisation of violence once took the form of mercenary armies marching under the flag of profit rather than state. Today it manifests in lines of code, algorithms, and proprietary platforms developed by corporations whose engineers, rather than generals, determine the strategies of conflict. The rise of artificial intelligence has introduced a new category of private military actor: the technology firm that builds autonomous weapons systems, cyberwarfare capabilities, or surveillance infrastructures and offers them to states in exchange for contracts. Unlike conventional arms manufacturers, these firms are not simply producing hardware. They are embedding decision-making authority into algorithms, shaping how wars are fought and how societies defend themselves, often without the transparency or accountability expected of governments. *The most unsettling dimension of this shift is that the boundary between public and private power is dissolving, leaving states dependent on corporations for the very tools that safeguard sovereignty.*

Consider Project Maven, the US Department of Defense's initiative to use AI to analyse drone footage. Initially developed in partnership with Google, it sparked internal dissent when employees protested against their work being used for warfare. Google eventually withdrew, but the programme continued with other firms, illustrating both the indispensability of private expertise and the fragility of corporate willingness. The state could not develop the capability on its own timeline, and the corporation could walk away, leaving national defence reliant on the shifting ethical stances of employees and boards. Here, the governance challenge becomes stark: who ultimately decides whether a nation fields a particular military technology—the elected representatives of its people, or the boardroom of a global technology company?

The partnerships are not limited to surveillance. Defence start-ups such as Anduril, founded by Palmer Luckey, are developing autonomous drones and border security systems with minimal government oversight in their early stages. Anduril's "Lattice" platform integrates data from multiple sensors to provide a live operating picture of battlefields and borders, effectively automating decision-making for defence operators. What distinguishes such companies from traditional contractors like Lockheed Martin is not merely their product range but their ethos: they are Silicon Valley firms applying venture-capital speed and risk appetite to the domain of national security. *The logic of disruption, so often celebrated in consumer markets, now applies to the waging of war.*

States are not passive in this transformation; they actively cultivate these relationships. The Pentagon's Defence Innovation Unit exists to bridge the gap between the military and start-ups, accelerating procurement and embedding private AI in national security infrastructure. The United Kingdom has launched partnerships with firms specialising in AI-driven cyber defence. Israel, long a leader in defence technology, has fostered a thriving ecosystem of AI firms developing offensive and defensive cyber tools, many of which are later sold abroad. Yet this deliberate entanglement carries costs: by leaning on private entities for national defence, states make themselves dependent on corporate stability, priorities, and values. A financial downturn in Silicon Valley or a leadership change in a major AI firm could ripple outward as a national security vulnerability.

The cyber domain magnifies these tensions further. Offensive cyber capabilities are often developed in collaboration with private contractors, blurring attribution and accountability. When state-backed hackers exploit vulnerabilities, the tools may originate in privately developed exploits. The case of the NSO Group and its Pegasus spyware illustrates how private actors can shape geopolitics. Marketed as a counterterrorism tool, Pegasus was found to be deployed against journalists, dissidents, and opposition figures worldwide. Governments purchased it, but its development and distribution were entirely corporate. Here the line between state abuse and corporate complicity collapses. *When a company has the power to surveil heads of state and civil society alike, its role transcends commerce; it becomes an unacknowledged player in international relations.*

Supporters of these partnerships argue that states cannot afford to forgo private expertise. The rapid pace of AI development outstrips the capacity of most bureaucracies. To compete with adversaries, they say, democracies must harness the dynamism of their private sectors. Indeed, the relative openness of the US technology ecosystem is often contrasted with China, where firms like Baidu or Huawei operate within a state-directed framework, aligning corporate goals with national strategy. In the Western context, however, this very openness generates strategic vulnerability. States may be forced to rely on firms whose incentives are not always aligned with national security, whose workforce may resist military projects, or whose global operations complicate questions of allegiance.

The philosophical question at the heart of this development concerns legitimacy. War and security have historically been the ultimate expression of state sovereignty. By outsourcing these functions to private firms, governments dilute their own moral authority over life-and-death decisions. Who is accountable when an AI-guided drone makes a mistake? When a cyberattack developed by a contractor escalates into international conflict, does responsibility rest with the commissioning state, the private developer, or both? The opacity of AI systems further muddies these waters. States may not even fully understand the workings of the tools they deploy, relying instead on vendor assurances. *The chain of accountability risks breaking precisely where it matters most—in decisions of violence and defence.*

There are also geopolitical consequences. Access to cutting-edge AI weaponry and cyber tools is mediated not only by states but by corporate partnerships. Smaller nations, unable to build these capabilities indigenously, must negotiate with firms that may prioritise profit or geopolitics over their security needs. This introduces a new layer of dependency in the global order. It is no longer sufficient to ask which states possess nuclear arsenals or advanced fighter jets; one must also ask which corporations are willing to provide, maintain, or deny access to digital arsenals. This corporate gatekeeping fragments traditional security alliances and creates channels of influence outside diplomatic treaties.

Some argue that this blurring of boundaries is not unprecedented. Private military contractors such as Blackwater in Iraq already demonstrated how warfare can be privatised. Yet the scale and scope of AI-driven militarisation differ fundamentally. A mercenary company can be dissolved, but an algorithm, once deployed, proliferates rapidly and may be copied or adapted without control. The dual-use nature of AI—equally applicable to civilian and military domains—means that innovations in one arena can quickly migrate to another. A natural language model designed for chat applications might also be used to generate phishing emails or disinformation at scale. *The same private laboratories driving consumer technology are, knowingly or not, equipping the arsenals of cyber conflict.*

The challenge for governance is profound. Traditional arms control treaties depend on clear categories of weapons, verifiable stockpiles, and state accountability. AI technologies defy these structures. They can be distributed digitally, modified easily, and deployed covertly. Even if states agreed to restrictions, private firms would remain outside many treaty frameworks, creating loopholes and enforcement dilemmas. Efforts to regulate autonomous weapons at the United Nations have stalled precisely because of these complexities, with corporations playing an informal but decisive role in shaping national positions.

This landscape calls for new political thinking. If private firms are indeed becoming "private militaries of code," then democratic societies must reconsider how they oversee the delegation of violence and defence. Mechanisms of accountability must extend beyond parliaments and ministries to include corporate actors whose products are integral to security. Transparency, oversight, and ethical standards cannot remain optional when the stakes are war and peace. Otherwise, the world risks entering a phase where conflict is not only privatised but automated, governed by algorithms optimised for efficiency rather than justice.

The blurring of state and corporate power in warfare represents not merely a technical or strategic shift but a redefinition of sovereignty itself. Just as the East India Company once blurred the line between commerce and empire, today's AI firms fuse profit with power in ways that challenge the very notion of who governs violence. The battlefield of the future will be as much a contest between algorithms and infrastructures as between armies and fleets, and the actors who shape it will not always be states. They will be corporations, armed with code, negotiating contracts that double as instruments of war.

Policy Capture and Dependence

Few developments in recent political history are as quietly transformative as the shift of sovereign decision-making from governments to corporate platforms. It is not an abstraction to say that technology companies now shape the daily experience of law and governance. Algorithms decide what information citizens encounter, infrastructures determine which voices are amplified or silenced, and platforms control how public services, from healthcare to taxation, are administered. What distinguishes this new form of influence is its depth: *nations are not merely influenced by corporate lobbying, they are increasingly governed by the infrastructures those corporations provide.* When states cannot function without private platforms, sovereignty itself becomes conditional on shareholder interests.

Consider the domain of digital identity. India's Aadhaar system, the world's largest biometric identification programme, is nominally a state initiative. Yet its functioning depends heavily on private contractors for database management, security protocols, and authentication services. A breach, error, or withdrawal of service by a private firm could compromise not just individual data but the integrity of a nationwide welfare system. Similarly, the United States relies on Amazon Web Services to host sensitive government data, including that of the CIA. In such cases, outsourcing is not about peripheral convenience but core state capacity. The choice to entrust infrastructure to corporations creates a dependency that rivals traditional geopolitical alliances. *When a government's ability to operate hinges on the stability of a private vendor, the boundary between public and private governance is fundamentally redrawn.*

The pandemic accelerated these dynamics. Governments turned to technology firms for vaccine distribution logistics, digital contact tracing, and remote education platforms. Apple and Google effectively set global standards for exposure notification by creating APIs that national health authorities had little choice but to adopt. No international treaty mandated their framework; no parliamentary vote determined its parameters. The governance of public health in a crisis was, in practice, dictated by two corporations headquartered in California. Their decisions were not arbitrary—there was a technical rationale—but they nonetheless demonstrate how, in moments of national urgency, state sovereignty can yield to corporate architecture.

Policy capture also occurs more subtly, through the shaping of regulatory environments. Platforms are not passive recipients of legislation; they actively design the conditions in which they operate. Microsoft's close involvement in drafting cybersecurity frameworks, or Facebook's lobbying efforts to influence content moderation rules in multiple jurisdictions, exemplify this phenomenon. States, under pressure to act swiftly in domains where they lack expertise, often accept industry-drafted solutions. The result is a paradox: regulation exists, but it reflects the interests of those it is supposed to constrain. *When the regulated write the rules, sovereignty becomes procedural theatre rather than substantive control.*

This dependence is not universal. China has pursued an alternative path by keeping core infrastructures under state dominance and subjecting domestic firms to strict party oversight. Western democracies, however, have chosen partnership and outsourcing. Proponents argue this model harnesses innovation and ensures responsiveness to changing technology. Critics respond that it entrenches asymmetry: governments, with their slower bureaucratic processes, cannot easily renegotiate terms once platforms are embedded. The balance of power is structural, not situational. A ministry may change its procurement policies, but a nation cannot simply replace the infrastructure that underpins its communications, its defence, or its economy without catastrophic disruption.

The European Union provides an instructive case. In attempting to regulate Big Tech through the Digital Services Act and Digital Markets Act, the EU seeks to reassert sovereignty over platforms. Yet the enforcement of such regulation still depends on cooperation from the very firms being regulated. Whether disinformation is removed, whether competition rules are followed, or whether user data is handled lawfully—all depend on the internal compliance mechanisms of multinational corporations. The EU's theoretical sovereignty is thus constantly mediated by private compliance officers and algorithmic systems, which may or may not align with the public interest.

The philosophical stakes are profound. Sovereignty has historically meant the capacity of a state to exercise authority over its territory and citizens without external constraint. But if the infrastructures of governance are owned and operated by corporations, that authority becomes contingent. This is not merely a problem of regulation but of ontology: what does it mean to govern, if the tools of governance are leased rather than owned? A government can legislate, but if its digital services fail because a corporation changes its terms of service, the law is impotent. *The architecture of power shifts from the parliament to the platform.*

There is also a democratic deficit. Shareholders in a technology company have no obligation to the citizens of the countries that depend on their platforms. Their fiduciary duty is to maximise returns, not to protect sovereignty. Yet their decisions have sovereign consequences. If a corporation discontinues a product line or alters a security protocol, it may destabilise a government's ability to deliver public services. Citizens, meanwhile, have no electoral recourse to influence these corporate decisions. The mechanisms of accountability that underpin democracy stop at the corporate firewall.

Real-world examples highlight this asymmetry with urgency. Twitter's sudden changes in content moderation policies under new ownership directly affected diplomatic communications, public health messaging, and the functioning of political opposition movements in fragile democracies. Such changes were not the result of national debates or international consensus but of unilateral corporate governance. Similarly, Meta's decision to withdraw news content in Canada during disputes over revenue-sharing laws demonstrated how corporate strategy can override the communicative fabric of a democracy. In both instances, sovereignty was not simply pressured but bypassed.

Some argue that states retain ultimate power: they can legislate, regulate, or nationalise. Yet this assertion overlooks the scale and complexity of modern platforms. Nationalisation may be theoretically possible but practically unfeasible, given the transnational operations and technical intricacies of firms like Google or Microsoft. Even if a state attempted to build alternatives, the global network effects of existing platforms would render them marginal. Sovereignty here becomes not absolute but negotiated, conditional, and at times illusory.

The danger is not merely dependency but capture. Policy decisions made in deference to corporate interests can redirect the trajectory of entire nations. Taxation frameworks adjusted to attract technology investment may limit fiscal capacity for decades. Content moderation standards designed by platforms shape civic discourse and political stability. Defence partnerships with AI firms influence military doctrine and the ethics of war. These are not auxiliary choices; they are constitutional in effect. *When states outsource decision-making to corporate platforms, they do not merely borrow tools—they reshape the meaning of sovereignty around corporate priorities.*

The dilemma is not solved by rejecting corporate involvement outright. The complexity and pace of technological change make collaboration inevitable. But collaboration need not mean submission. The challenge for states is to design mechanisms that ensure partnerships serve public sovereignty rather than shareholder profit. This requires not only regulatory innovation but also cultural recognition: sovereignty in the digital age cannot be exercised without attention to the infrastructures that mediate it. To ignore this reality is to accept a future where governments legislate in theory but corporations govern in fact.

When Corporates Dictate Diplomacy

Diplomacy has always been the preserve of states, with emissaries, treaties, and summits functioning as the stage upon which national interests are negotiated. Yet in the age of artificial intelligence, corporations increasingly enter that stage not as background actors but as decisive participants. The emergence of AI firms as de facto diplomats is not merely symbolic. Their technologies structure negotiations, set the parameters of what is possible, and sometimes constrain states in ways that diplomats themselves cannot. This is a profound shift: *trade agreements and international policies are now being shaped not only in ministries and embassies but also in corporate boardrooms and research labs.*

The influence of AI corporations in diplomacy is best understood through the lens of dependency. Nations that rely on foreign technology firms for critical AI systems effectively import a new layer of political vulnerability. For instance, when OpenAI restricts access to its cutting-edge models due to concerns about misuse, entire regions are excluded from technological frontiers. This exclusion is not a matter of tariffs or sanctions, but of a corporate decision framed in terms of ethics and safety. Yet the geopolitical effect is identical to a policy embargo: it shapes who has access to the engines of economic growth, and who is left trailing. Countries dependent on these technologies find themselves lobbying not just other governments but also the corporations themselves, making the latter indispensable nodes in global diplomacy.

Trade negotiations illustrate this vividly. In discussions over digital trade provisions within agreements like the Comprehensive and Progressive Agreement for Trans-Pacific Partnership (CPTPP) or the United States–Mexico–Canada Agreement (USMCA), corporations such as Microsoft and Google are not passive observers. Their lobbying shapes the legal frameworks around data localisation, cross-border data flows, and intellectual property rights. When governments attempt to regulate the flow of sensitive data, these firms mobilise diplomatic pressure through their host states, creating a triangle where corporate interests, national policy, and international negotiations are interwoven. *It is no longer possible to disentangle state diplomacy from corporate strategy when the infrastructure of trade itself is digital and corporately owned.*

Consider the contest over AI standards. The International Telecommunication Union (ITU), a United Nations body, has been a forum where China, the United States, and European countries debate ethical and technical frameworks for AI. Yet alongside these state representatives sit corporate delegates whose technical submissions often become the default standards. Huawei's proposed frameworks for facial recognition, for example, were not simply contributions but attempts to embed a commercial advantage within international norms. Similarly, American firms such as IBM and Microsoft have influenced debates on responsible AI by offering ethical principles that double as strategic defences against more onerous regulation. Here diplomacy is not only about states agreeing but about corporations codifying their interests into the rules of international governance.

There are moments when corporate decisions directly shift the tenor of international relations. When Google withdrew from China in 2010, citing censorship and cyberattacks, the move was widely interpreted as a diplomatic rupture as much as a business decision. The withdrawal altered the technological landscape of the world's second-largest economy, catalysed the growth of domestic champions like Baidu and Tencent, and hardened the divide between Western and Chinese digital ecosystems. A single corporate exit reverberated like a geopolitical sanction. It signalled to governments and diplomats alike that the strategies of corporations could redraw spheres of influence.

More recently, export controls on advanced semiconductors and AI chips, imposed by the United States on China, reveal another layer of complexity. While these are state-led restrictions, enforcement depends heavily on corporate compliance by firms such as Nvidia and ASML. The diplomatic struggle between Washington and Beijing is mediated through the willingness of corporations to align with government strategy. In this case, corporations act simultaneously as instruments of statecraft and as self-interested actors negotiating carve-outs to protect revenue streams. The result is a form of diplomacy in which national policies are negotiated with the tacit participation of corporations, who may resist or recalibrate their operations based on market incentives.

This dual role—where corporations are both subjects and agents of diplomacy—creates friction. For smaller nations, negotiating access to AI technologies means navigating not just the interests of the United States, Europe, or China, but also those of individual corporations. African nations seeking equitable AI access, for example, must contend with the fact that most foundational models are developed and controlled by Western firms. International development agreements in digital infrastructure, often brokered by institutions like the World Bank, are therefore inseparable from the licensing terms of Google Cloud, Amazon Web Services, or Microsoft Azure. What appears as intergovernmental aid may, in practice, be a channel for corporate dominance, giving firms enduring leverage over national economies.

Diplomatic asymmetry is also evident in the regulation of online platforms. The European Union's attempts to enforce antitrust laws and data protection under the General Data Protection Regulation (GDPR) have triggered diplomatic disputes with the United States, where many technology firms are headquartered. Here corporations play the role of contested territory: they are private entities, but their compliance or resistance has implications for national sovereignty and international relations. When Meta threatened to withdraw services from Europe if regulatory frameworks proved too burdensome, it was not simply a negotiation between a regulator and a company—it became a matter of transatlantic diplomacy, with governments intervening on behalf of "their" corporations.

Critics argue that the growing corporate role in diplomacy undermines democratic accountability. Traditional diplomacy, for all its opacity, is at least theoretically tied to public interest through elected governments. Corporate diplomacy, by contrast, is tethered to shareholder value. When a corporation influences trade negotiations or dictates technological access, its calculations are financial, not civic. *The ethical stakes of international relations are thus refracted through balance sheets rather than constitutions.* Yet defenders contend that corporations bring indispensable technical expertise and speed to diplomatic processes that would otherwise lag years behind technological change. Without corporate input, treaties and agreements risk being irrelevant upon signing.

The truth lies somewhere in between. Corporations have become indispensable to diplomacy precisely because they own and operate the infrastructures of the digital age. AI systems are not neutral tools; they embody values, priorities, and architectures that determine how states interact. A government negotiating climate agreements must consider not only carbon targets but also the AI-driven energy systems that optimise national grids, many of which are controlled by private firms. Similarly, military alliances now incorporate corporate partners to integrate AI-enabled logistics, surveillance, and cyber capabilities. Diplomacy no longer occurs solely across the table between foreign ministers. It happens in contracts, APIs, and licensing agreements that bind states to corporate platforms as tightly as any treaty.

The entanglement of corporate AI systems with diplomacy raises a difficult philosophical question: *who speaks for humanity in an age where the infrastructures of knowledge and power are privately owned?* States claim to represent their citizens, but when they must defer to corporations for access to essential technologies, representation becomes diluted. Diplomacy is redefined as a three-sided process where states negotiate not only with each other but with firms whose reach transcends borders. The Westphalian system, premised on state sovereignty, strains under the weight of corporate influence. If diplomacy is the art of negotiating power, then the twenty-first century has introduced new diplomats—CEOs, engineers, and platform architects—whose authority is unelected yet unavoidable.

The case studies of AI's impact on diplomacy make one truth inescapable: the balance of power is shifting. What once required embassies and treaties can now be reshaped by a change in a corporation's terms of service, or by the selective granting of access to an AI system. The map of international relations is being redrawn not just by military alliances or economic blocs, but by the strategic decisions of private firms whose algorithms mediate communication, trade, and governance. For readers seeking to understand the future of diplomacy, the essential insight is that corporations no longer whisper in the ears of states—they dictate the terms upon which states can even enter the conversation.

Chapter 7

Cultural Blind Spots

The claim that algorithms are neutral arbiters of truth has become one of the most enduring myths of the digital age. The promise of objectivity is seductive: a belief that code, written in the language of mathematics, can transcend human prejudice. Yet algorithms are not born in abstraction; they are trained on the residue of human culture. They learn from data that is itself encoded with history, hierarchy, and bias. Far from being impartial, artificial intelligence mirrors the inequities of the societies that produce it, embedding cultural preferences into seemingly universal systems. What is presented as neutral is often the subtle imposition of one worldview over another, wrapped in the authority of technology. To understand AI, then, is to interrogate the cultural assumptions beneath its surface, the invisible scaffolding that shapes how machines see the world and, by extension, how they make decisions about ours.

The most immediate blind spot is the myth of neutrality itself. Consider facial recognition systems, which consistently perform less accurately on darker-skinned individuals, particularly women. This discrepancy is not an accident of coding but the result of training data dominated by lighter-skinned faces, drawn disproportionately from Western populations. In practice, the algorithm's 'vision' is conditioned by the cultural and demographic realities of those who built it. When exported globally, these systems do not simply misrecognise—they impose a hierarchy of visibility, where certain bodies are legible and others marginal. The myth of neutrality thus serves as a shield, allowing the reproduction of cultural inequality while presenting itself as scientific inevitability. *Algorithms are not abstract logic; they are social artefacts, encoded with choices about what matters and what does not.*

But if algorithms are not neutral, whose values do they serve? The contest here is unmistakably geopolitical. On one side, Western firms often embed assumptions aligned with liberal individualism: the sanctity of privacy, the rights of the consumer, and the primacy of the market. On the other, authoritarian models emphasise collective security, surveillance, and the subordination of individual freedoms to state stability. A social media recommendation system designed in California implicitly privileges freedom of expression and engagement metrics, whereas a similar platform in Beijing may optimise for political conformity and national cohesion. The code is not merely technical—it is normative, exporting cultural visions of how societies should function. Trade agreements, technological standards, and software licences become the vehicles through which these values travel, shaping the governance structures of nations far from the original point of design.

This raises a troubling question: can global AI truly be plural when its architecture is so heavily shaped by dominant powers? The spread of AI systems mirrors older patterns of cultural imperialism, where powerful nations exported not just goods but ways of life. Today, the code that underpins predictive policing, financial algorithms, or health diagnostics is often written in Silicon Valley or Shenzhen, then deployed across cities in Africa, Latin America, or Southeast Asia. While the interfaces may localise—adapting language or currency—the underlying logic carries the imprint of its origin. *The cultural blind spot is that what feels universal is often provincial: a local value system dressed in the authority of global technology.*

Yet resistance is emerging from those unwilling to accept homogenisation. Indigenous communities, for example, have begun to assert digital sovereignty, demanding that their cultural practices and epistemologies be reflected in AI systems that touch their lives. In Canada, some First Nations groups are experimenting with data sovereignty frameworks to ensure that health and demographic information is stored and processed in ways consistent with their traditions, rather than subsumed into Western-centric models of governance. In New Zealand, Māori scholars are raising concerns about how AI systems classify language, knowledge, and identity, pushing instead for technologies that support the revitalisation of te reo Māori and indigenous storytelling. These movements remind us that cultural resistance does not always take the form of rejecting technology; it often involves reshaping it, embedding pluralism into the very fabric of digital systems.

The struggle against homogenisation is not only collective but deeply personal. AI systems shape identities at both the individual and societal level, influencing how people see themselves and how they are seen by others. Recommendation engines curate cultural consumption, from the music we hear to the news we read, creating feedback loops that reinforce certain aspects of identity while marginalising others. For diasporic communities, these systems can be double-edged: offering connection to heritage while simultaneously flattening it into consumable categories defined by external algorithms. A young Ghanaian in London might find Afrobeat recommended to them by Spotify's algorithm, but the platform's categorisation of "African music" often compresses diverse traditions into a single bucket. Identity becomes an artefact of how machines parse culture, constrained by the limits of their training sets.

The stakes are even higher at the collective level. National identities are increasingly mediated through AI systems that rank, sort, and filter information. A state that relies on foreign AI for information infrastructure may find its cultural narratives subtly shaped by external coding choices. Imagine a government deploying an AI system for educational curricula, only to discover that the knowledge prioritised reflects the biases of its developers rather than the needs of its citizens. The implications are not abstract: they affect how young people see their past, their language, and their place in the world. *When algorithms shape identity, they do not just curate preference—they redraw the boundaries of belonging.*

Critically, cultural blind spots are not always intentional. Developers often believe they are building universal tools, only to later discover how narrow their assumptions were. A translation algorithm trained primarily on European languages might stumble over African tonal systems, not out of malice but neglect. Yet neglect itself is political. It reveals who is considered worth including and who is relegated to the margins. The danger lies not in deliberate domination alone, but in the quiet erasures that occur when the data does not capture the fullness of human diversity. Cultural blind spots are not always overt acts of power; they are often the absence of recognition, the silence where alternative ways of knowing should be.

For professionals and policymakers, acknowledging these blind spots is not a matter of cultural sensitivity alone but of strategic necessity. An AI system that fails to account for local context can trigger diplomatic disputes, spark mistrust, or even destabilise fragile societies. When predictive policing tools imported from the United States were trialled in European cities, they ran into public backlash over civil liberties. When language models trained on Western corpora are used in regions with different moral codes, they can generate outputs deemed offensive or illegitimate. Such failures erode confidence in technology, undermining both political stability and commercial viability. Cultural blind spots, in other words, are not only ethical vulnerabilities but practical liabilities.

The challenge ahead is to move from a monoculture of code to a pluralism of design. This requires not just technical adjustments but political will: international frameworks that respect cultural sovereignty, corporate practices that engage with diverse communities, and educational systems that train developers to recognise their own positionality. It also demands humility, an admission that no algorithm can be fully neutral, that every line of code carries a lineage of values and assumptions. *The recognition of cultural blind spots is the first step towards building technologies that truly serve humanity in its plurality, rather than imposing the narrowness of the few upon the many.*

As this chapter unfolds, it will trace these dimensions with depth and clarity: how the myth of neutrality hides encoded hierarchies, how competing political systems export their values through code, how local movements resist algorithmic homogenisation, and how identity itself is reconfigured by machines that claim to know us. The reader will come to see that culture is not an afterthought of AI but one of its most contested battlegrounds. To overlook this is to misunderstand the essence of our technological age. To confront it is to open the possibility of a digital future that honours the diversity of human life rather than erasing it.

The Myth of Neutrality

The conviction that algorithms stand outside human bias has been one of the most powerful illusions of the digital era. Numbers, after all, appear incorruptible. Code is written in formal logic, and machine learning systems calculate patterns from vast oceans of data. What could be more objective? Yet the apparent purity of mathematics conceals a profound truth: algorithms are shaped by the imperfections of the world from which they learn. Far from being impartial, they often replicate—and even amplify—the cultural hierarchies embedded in their training data. The neutrality of algorithms is not a scientific fact but a cultural narrative, a myth that masks power behind the façade of technical inevitability.

Consider the now well-documented failures of facial recognition technology. Studies by researchers such as Joy Buolamwini at MIT demonstrated that widely deployed commercial systems from major technology companies consistently misclassified women and people with darker skin tones at far higher rates than white men. These systems were not designed to discriminate consciously, but they had been trained on datasets overwhelmingly dominated by lighter-skinned, male faces. The algorithm, therefore, 'learnt' a world in which whiteness and masculinity were default categories. The errors were not minor inconveniences: they had consequences for policing, border security, and public trust. The claim that the algorithm was neutral fell apart once it became clear that it was, in fact, entrenching a hierarchy of visibility. Some faces were recognised as legitimate identities; others were treated as statistical noise. *Bias in training data becomes bias in social reality when deployed at scale.*

The myth of neutrality persists partly because it is convenient. Technology companies can position themselves as providers of objective tools, not political actors. Governments, too, often find neutrality a useful fiction, allowing them to outsource contentious decisions to 'the algorithm' rather than confront the underlying value judgments those decisions entail. When an automated welfare system denies benefits, it is easier to claim the system followed impartial rules than to admit those rules were designed with assumptions about who deserves assistance. Neutrality, then, functions less as a description of algorithms than as a shield against accountability. *The danger lies not only in the presence of bias but in the denial that bias exists at all.*

Some defenders of algorithmic neutrality argue that bias is simply a technical problem: expand the dataset, refine the model, and neutrality can be restored. While this approach may improve performance, it risks obscuring deeper structural issues. Training data is not a mirror of objective reality; it is a mirror of existing human behaviour, which is itself shaped by inequities. Predictive policing tools, for instance, often reinforce racial disparities because their training data comes from historical arrest records. If certain communities have been over-policed for decades, the data will reflect higher arrest rates there, teaching the algorithm that crime is more likely to occur in those areas. The result is a feedback loop: the system sends more police to those communities, generates more arrests, and strengthens the original bias. Neutrality cannot be achieved by scaling up the data when the data itself encodes injustice.

Moreover, neutrality is undermined not only by bias in training data but by the very act of choosing what to optimise. Every algorithm has an objective function: maximise engagement, minimise risk, predict recidivism. These goals are not given by nature; they are selected by developers, corporations, or governments, often reflecting commercial or political priorities. A recommendation system designed to maximise time on platform implicitly values user attention as a commodity, even if it comes at the cost of spreading misinformation or polarisation. A loan approval algorithm that seeks to minimise default risk implicitly places profit above equitable access to credit. To claim neutrality here is to ignore that *every optimisation is a value choice, every metric a reflection of what matters to those in power.*

One of the most striking aspects of algorithmic neutrality as myth is its cultural asymmetry. Systems built in one part of the world often carry assumptions that do not translate seamlessly elsewhere. For example, sentiment analysis algorithms trained predominantly on English-language corpora may misinterpret irony, sarcasm, or culturally specific forms of expression in other languages. In some cases, they may categorise neutral or even positive statements in non-Western dialects as negative simply because they do not fit the linguistic norms of the training data. Similarly, content moderation systems developed in the United States frequently struggle with context in regions such as Myanmar or Ethiopia, where local political speech patterns are unfamiliar to Silicon Valley engineers. Here the myth of neutrality operates not only as denial of bias but as cultural imperialism: local realities are misjudged, distorted, or silenced by global systems that claim universality.

Philosophically, the myth rests on a misunderstanding of what it means for knowledge to be objective. Objectivity does not mean absence of perspective; it means accountability to multiple perspectives. True neutrality would require algorithms to incorporate diverse cultural vantage points and to expose their assumptions to scrutiny. Yet most AI systems are designed within narrow institutional and cultural contexts, often by relatively homogeneous teams. This lack of diversity is not incidental but systemic. It reflects who has access to the education, resources, and corporate environments where cutting-edge AI is built. The neutrality of the algorithm, then, is an illusion sustained by a lack of transparency about whose perspectives are embedded in the code.

There are also significant tensions in public perception. For many users, the allure of neutrality lies in trust: the belief that algorithms can make fairer decisions than flawed humans. This belief is not entirely misplaced. In some domains, such as medical diagnostics, AI systems have demonstrated higher accuracy than human practitioners, particularly in detecting early signs of cancer in imaging. Yet even here, the neutrality narrative is misleading. The success of these systems depends on the populations from which their training data is drawn. An AI diagnostic tool trained primarily on European medical datasets may perform less effectively on African or Asian populations, not because it is less intelligent but because it has not been exposed to sufficient variation. The neutrality myth, by masking these limitations, risks fostering misplaced confidence.

The question, then, is not whether algorithms can ever be neutral, but how societies should grapple with the fact that they are not. One response is greater transparency: opening datasets and models to independent scrutiny, so biases can be identified and addressed. Another is diversity in design: ensuring that development teams and governance structures represent a range of cultural and social backgrounds. But perhaps most importantly, there must be a shift in how neutrality itself is understood. It should not be treated as a given state that algorithms can achieve through technical refinement, but as an ongoing negotiation of values, perspectives, and trade-offs. Neutrality is not the absence of bias but the conscious effort to make biases visible and accountable.

The persistence of the neutrality myth reveals something about human psychology. We want to believe that technology can deliver what politics cannot: fairness without conflict, order without debate. But in reality, algorithms inherit the same complexities that mark human societies. They reflect choices about whose data to collect, whose voices to prioritise, and whose interests to serve. To dismantle the myth of neutrality is not to condemn algorithms as irredeemably biased but to accept that they are *tools of culture as much as tools of science.* Recognising this truth allows for a more honest conversation about how to build systems that respect pluralism rather than conceal domination under the veil of mathematics.

The deeper lesson is that neutrality has always been a political claim, not a technical one. Just as the maps of empires once presented certain territories as empty or peripheral, so too do algorithms today render some people invisible and others central. By exposing the myth of neutrality, we confront the reality that algorithms are instruments of power. The task, then, is not to search for neutrality where it cannot exist, but to insist on accountability where power is exercised. Only then can we begin to imagine AI systems that do not merely replicate cultural hierarchies but challenge them, creating spaces where multiple forms of knowledge and identity can coexist.

Whose Values Rule?

Artificial intelligence is often described as a universal technology, a set of systems built upon mathematical principles that transcend borders. Yet beneath the technical architecture lie choices—about what data to include, which objectives to optimise, and which values to privilege. These choices are never value-free. They carry within them political assumptions, moral commitments, and cultural orientations. The global spread of AI therefore, raises a profound question: when algorithms mediate social life, *whose values are being exported through the code?*

The contrast is most visible between two dominant centres of AI development: the United States and China. In the United States, AI systems are largely shaped by commercial incentives rooted in liberal capitalism. Silicon Valley companies optimise algorithms for engagement, growth, and profit. Platforms such as Facebook and YouTube design recommendation engines that maximise user attention, reinforcing the cultural priority placed on individual choice and consumer freedom—even when those choices lead to misinformation, polarisation, or addictive behaviour. The American narrative positions AI as an extension of liberal democracy: innovation flourishes in a competitive marketplace, and individual users are empowered to decide how they engage with digital systems. Yet the very emphasis on personal freedom embeds a cultural assumption: that liberty is best exercised through consumer choice, and that the protection of speech outweighs the risks of harm.

In China, by contrast, AI development is guided by state-directed priorities. Algorithms are designed to reinforce collective stability, national security, and social order. The widespread use of facial recognition in public surveillance, or the application of social credit systems, reflects a different cultural logic: the individual is seen as inseparable from the collective, and the legitimacy of personal expression is measured against its contribution to social harmony. AI is not an arena for unregulated competition but a tool of governance, deployed to strengthen the party-state's authority. Here, the values embedded in code reflect authoritarian collectivism rather than liberal individualism. Where American systems monetise attention, Chinese systems discipline behaviour.

Neither model is neutral, and both raise concerns. The Western emphasis on profit-driven optimisation has led to platforms whose algorithms fuel polarisation, amplifying extreme voices because they generate more engagement. The Chinese emphasis on state control, meanwhile, threatens personal autonomy and freedom of thought, with algorithms used to predict and pre-empt dissent. What emerges is not a universal AI but a geopolitical contest of value-laden systems, each exporting its own vision of human order. Nations adopting American-built platforms inherit the logic of consumer freedom and shareholder profit; those turning to

Chinese infrastructure often import a model of centralised surveillance and conformity.

The export of values through code is not always explicit. It often happens quietly, through the technical design of systems. Consider natural language processing models. Many of the most powerful language models are trained predominantly on English-language sources, reflecting Western cultural assumptions, idioms, and conceptual frameworks. When these models are deployed globally, they privilege certain modes of expression and marginalise others. Words, metaphors, and moral categories specific to non-Western cultures may be mistranslated, misinterpreted, or rendered invisible. In this way, linguistic hierarchies are inscribed into the very infrastructure of AI, subtly reproducing cultural dominance under the guise of technical sophistication.

At the same time, local actors are not passive recipients of foreign values. Governments and corporations adapt imported AI to their own contexts, sometimes bending it to reinforce local ideologies. Social media platforms in authoritarian states, for instance, may adopt American-built recommendation systems but modify them to censor politically sensitive content. Conversely, democratic societies deploying Chinese-made surveillance technologies often impose legal constraints that limit their scope. *Values travel with code, but they are also contested, translated, and reinterpreted along the way.* The global AI landscape is thus a site of negotiation, where competing cultural norms are embedded, resisted, or hybridised through technology.

It is tempting to imagine that technical standards might offer a way out—that if AI systems were developed under international guidelines, they could transcend these cultural divisions. Yet standards themselves are political. The debate over facial recognition regulation in the European Union illustrates this tension. European policymakers have sought to balance innovation with human rights, framing AI governance through the lens of dignity, privacy, and proportionality. These principles reflect Europe's historical experience with authoritarian regimes and its philosophical traditions of humanism. By contrast, both American and Chinese approaches have been more pragmatic, focusing on economic competitiveness and national security. What counts as 'ethical AI' is therefore not a universal category but an expression of political culture.

The struggle over values in AI also extends into domains less visible to the public. Trade negotiations increasingly include clauses about data governance, source code disclosure, and cross-border data flows. These provisions, though technical, are battles over values: whether data should be treated as a commodity subject to free trade, as in the American vision, or as a sovereign resource to be tightly controlled, as in the Chinese and increasingly European view. When countries sign such agreements, they are not only committing to economic terms but aligning themselves with a particular vision of digital sovereignty and cultural order.

This raises a deeper philosophical question: can AI ever be truly pluralist, or must it always encode the values of its designers? To some extent, algorithms can be localised, incorporating culturally specific datasets or tailoring optimisation functions to local priorities. Yet the infrastructure of AI—its architectures, training methods, and platforms—is often dominated by a handful of global corporations and state-backed initiatives. This concentration of power makes it difficult for alternative cultural models to flourish at scale. Indigenous or minority communities seeking to build AI systems that reflect their own values often lack the resources to compete. *The danger is that AI becomes a homogenising force, spreading the values of the powerful under the illusion of technical inevitability.*

There are, however, signs of resistance. Initiatives in Africa, Latin America, and parts of Asia are pushing for AI systems that reflect local epistemologies and social needs. For example, projects that use AI to support indigenous language preservation challenge the dominance of English-centric models. Efforts to design agricultural AI tailored to smallholder farmers in sub-Saharan Africa resist the one-size-fits-all solutions of global corporations. These movements remind us that the values embedded in AI are not fixed but subject to contestation. They open the possibility of digital pluralism: a world where multiple cultural visions of technology coexist, rather than one hegemonic model dictating the rules.

The question of whose values rule, then, is not a technical puzzle to be solved but a political reality to be navigated. Algorithms are not abstract engines of logic but embodiments of cultural choice. They reflect whether a society prioritises freedom or stability, profit or justice, individuality or collectivity. To treat them as neutral tools is to obscure the power relations they sustain. Recognising their value-laden nature allows for a more honest global conversation: not about whether AI should carry values, but about *which values we are willing to inscribe into the systems that increasingly govern human life.*

The stakes are high. As AI continues to mediate economic exchange, political communication, and social identity, the values embedded in its design will shape the contours of global order. Whether the future tilts towards the commercial logics of Silicon Valley, the authoritarian collectivism of Beijing, or a more pluralist constellation of cultural visions, will depend not only on technical innovation but on political will. The myth of neutrality has already been dispelled; the real task is to decide whose values are allowed to rule.

Resistance Through Culture

The story of artificial intelligence is often told as a march of inevitability: powerful technologies developed in the West or China, exported to the rest of the world, and adopted wholesale in the name of progress. Yet beneath this narrative of homogenisation lies a quieter, more contested reality. Across indigenous communities, small nations, and local grassroots movements, resistance is mounting against the flattening effects of algorithmic systems that erase cultural difference. These movements insist that technology should not merely extend the reach of dominant powers, but must adapt to, respect, and sustain diverse ways of life. *Digital pluralism emerges here not as a theoretical aspiration, but as a lived demand from communities fighting to protect their identity in the face of algorithmic standardisation.*

One of the most striking illustrations comes from the struggle to preserve indigenous languages. Commercial AI models, trained predominantly on English and other globally dominant tongues, tend to marginalise languages spoken by smaller populations. When speech recognition systems fail to recognise Māori, Quechua, or Navajo, the practical effect is to silence those voices in the digital domain. Resistance has taken the form of locally developed projects that use AI to revitalise, rather than erase, minority languages. In New Zealand, Māori technologists have partnered with researchers to build speech datasets that capture native pronunciation, ensuring that voice assistants and transcription tools can understand te reo Māori. Far from being a mere technical fix, this work represents a political act: it asserts the right of a community to exist digitally on its own terms, rather than being assimilated into the linguistic defaults of global corporations.

Similar dynamics are unfolding in Africa, where data scarcity in local languages often leads to exclusion. Large language models trained predominantly on European languages reinforce colonial hierarchies of knowledge, privileging Western modes of thought and communication.

The Masakhane project, an open, grassroots research initiative across the continent, seeks to counter this trend by developing natural language processing tools for African languages. Thousands of volunteers contribute to building datasets and translation systems that serve local needs, guided by the principle that Africans should be co-creators of the AI that affects them. *Here, resistance is not expressed through outright rejection of technology, but through a demand for meaningful participation in shaping its direction.*

The struggle extends beyond language to the cultural logic embedded in algorithmic systems. Recommendation algorithms on global platforms often elevate content that conforms to Western commercial sensibilities, sidelining local traditions, artistic forms, or political discourse. In Latin America, for instance, indigenous musicians have voiced concerns that YouTube's recommendation systems bury their work under globalised pop music, even when local audiences seek it out. The algorithm's definition of popularity encodes an implicit hierarchy: what counts as valuable is what generates the highest engagement on a global scale, not what sustains cultural continuity within a community. Local collectives have responded by creating independent platforms for distributing indigenous art, resisting not only the technical biases of the algorithm but the cultural assumptions that underpin it.

Some of the most consequential cultural pushback comes in the domain of data sovereignty. For many indigenous groups, data about their land, traditions, or health carries profound cultural significance and cannot be treated as a mere commodity. Yet corporate AI models often extract data indiscriminately, folding it into systems designed for global optimisation. In response, the Indigenous Data Sovereignty movement has developed the CARE principles—Collective benefit, Authority to control, Responsibility, and Ethics—as a counter to the Western FAIR principles of data sharing. This shift highlights a clash of values: while FAIR promotes openness and accessibility, CARE emphasises the rights of communities to govern how their data is used. The assertion is clear: algorithms trained on data without respecting cultural ownership perpetuate a form of digital colonialism, and resistance requires embedding indigenous ethics into the infrastructure of AI.

The case of the Sami people in northern Europe illustrates the stakes. Long subject to cultural erasure, the Sami have recently begun to assert control over how digital tools represent their environment and knowledge. When AI systems are used to model land for resource extraction, they often ignore traditional Sami understandings of ecology. Resistance takes the form of insisting that any technological model of the land must integrate indigenous knowledge systems, not merely treat them as anecdotal. In this sense, resistance through culture is not only about safeguarding heritage but about expanding what counts as legitimate knowledge in the age of algorithms.

Yet cultural resistance is not confined to indigenous groups. Small states and local institutions also push back against algorithmic homogenisation. The European Union's approach to AI governance, though rooted in Western liberal traditions, can be seen as a form of cultural resistance to the commercial logic of Silicon Valley. By foregrounding human dignity and privacy in legislation such as the General Data Protection Regulation (GDPR), Europe asserts its cultural memory of authoritarian surveillance as a counterweight to unrestrained data capitalism. Similarly, Singapore's emphasis on AI as a tool for social cohesion, rather than merely profit generation, reflects a local attempt to assert control over the values embedded in technology. While not indigenous in the narrow sense, these examples illustrate a broader pattern: communities seek to resist the uncritical adoption of AI logics that flatten their particular histories and priorities.

A recurring tension emerges here. On the one hand, the globalisation of AI promises access to powerful tools that can advance education, healthcare, and economic opportunity. On the other, those tools often arrive packaged with assumptions about how societies should function. Resistance through culture does not deny the value of AI, but demands that it be reinterpreted in ways that affirm local autonomy. The struggle is therefore not between tradition and modernity, but between homogenisation and pluralism. *The central claim is that diversity of culture must extend into the digital domain, or else the world risks reproducing historical patterns of domination through new technological means.*

The philosophical implications run deep. If algorithms are designed to optimise for efficiency, engagement, or prediction, what happens to values that prioritise memory, ritual, or community over optimisation? Indigenous resistance shows that cultural flourishing is not always measurable in clicks, conversions, or outputs. By challenging the very metrics through which algorithms define success, these movements invite a broader rethinking of what technology is for. Is AI a tool to accelerate global uniformity, or can it be reimagined as an instrument for sustaining multiplicity?

This resistance also exposes the limits of the narrative that sees AI as purely global. In practice, the local always intrudes: the cultural contexts in which algorithms operate determine their legitimacy and effectiveness. A recommendation system that seems neutral in California may be perceived as corrosive in Kenya; a biometric system praised for efficiency in Shanghai may be experienced as oppressive in Sámi territory. Recognising this means accepting that *there is no single universal path for AI development.* Resistance through culture demonstrates that legitimacy in technology must be negotiated at the intersection of global infrastructures and local identities.

What unites these diverse movements—from Māori language preservation to African data initiatives to European regulatory frameworks—is a shared refusal to accept algorithmic homogenisation as destiny. They reveal that the supposed universality of AI is an illusion, masking the dominance of a few cultural paradigms. By insisting on digital pluralism, these actors not only protect their own traditions but also enrich the global technological ecosystem. The future of AI, if it is to be just and sustainable, must be polyphonic rather than monolithic, drawing strength from the plurality of cultures it serves rather than erasing them in the pursuit of seamless optimisation.

Identity in the Machine

Few forces in contemporary life shape how we understand ourselves as powerfully as artificial intelligence. Identity, once anchored in the relatively slow-moving realms of culture, family, and nation, is increasingly mediated by algorithmic systems that anticipate our preferences, filter our choices, and even define the categories through which society perceives us. The tension lies in the fact that these systems are built upon globalised datasets, encoding patterns of behaviour that often flatten the unique contours of heritage, language, and memory. *To live within the reach of AI is to negotiate a constant dialogue between the inheritance of culture and the imperatives of code.*

Consider the way recommender systems on social media influence how individuals present themselves. A young artist in Lagos, for instance, may discover that art rooted in local folklore receives little algorithmic amplification compared to digital imitations of Western styles that match the preferences of global audiences. The result is an implicit nudge towards self-fashioning that aligns with dominant cultural aesthetics rather than local heritage. This is not simply about exposure or visibility; it is about the subtle reconfiguration of identity itself. When algorithms reward particular forms of expression, they help determine which identities feel viable in public space and which risk being marginalised into obscurity.

The dynamic is equally evident in the realm of language. AI-powered translation tools and large language models often prioritise globally dominant tongues such as English, Mandarin, or Spanish, while smaller languages struggle to find representation in digital systems. A speaker of Inuktitut or Basque may find that their words are consistently misinterpreted or excluded from digital interactions. Over time, this lack of recognition seeps into identity, reinforcing a sense that to participate fully in the modern digital sphere requires abandoning aspects of one's linguistic heritage. Resistance to this homogenising tendency is growing, with grassroots projects building AI tools specifically tailored to minority languages, yet the asymmetry remains striking: *identity is reshaped not by overt suppression, but by the quiet gravitational pull of globalised code.*

At the collective level, AI creates new categories through which groups are understood. Facial recognition systems, for example, are not merely neutral tools for identification. They embed cultural assumptions about what constitutes a "normal" face. Numerous studies have revealed that these systems perform more accurately on lighter skin tones, reflecting biases in the datasets on which they were trained. For communities systematically misrecognised, the effect is more than technical inconvenience; it is a message about belonging. If a system struggles to "see" you correctly, it signals that your identity is peripheral to the imagined centre of technological progress. In this way, AI both reflects and reinforces hierarchies of recognition, shaping collective identity through differential visibility.

The influence extends into the realm of aspiration. AI-driven career platforms, hiring algorithms, and educational recommendation systems often guide individuals towards opportunities based on patterns of prior success. This may appear efficient, but it risks reproducing structural inequities by narrowing the range of imagined futures. A student from a rural background may be algorithmically nudged away from advanced scientific fields simply because the data suggests fewer people with her profile succeed there. Her sense of identity—what she believes is possible for herself—is therefore curtailed not by personal failure, but by the inertia of machine-learned patterns. *Identity, in this sense, is not only about who we are, but about what futures we are allowed to conceive as plausible.*

Yet the story is not solely one of imposition. For some, AI systems enable new forms of identity that would have been unthinkable in earlier generations. Online spaces facilitated by algorithmic curation provide platforms for marginalised groups—LGBTQ+ communities, for example—to connect and share experiences across national and cultural boundaries. Here, the globalised nature of code becomes a resource rather than a threat, allowing identities to flourish that local cultural traditions may have suppressed. The paradox is clear: the same algorithmic architectures that homogenise expression in some contexts can liberate it in others. The determining factor is often whose values are embedded in the design and what kinds of plurality the system allows.

Philosophically, the emergence of identity in the machine raises profound questions about authenticity. If algorithms constantly predict our preferences and shape the options available, how do we distinguish between desires that are truly our own and those subtly manufactured by predictive systems? When a streaming service anticipates the next song we "want" to hear, or an e-commerce site offers the product we are "likely" to buy, the line between autonomous choice and algorithmic suggestion blurs. *Identity risks becoming not a discovery of self, but a reflection of feedback loops optimised for engagement.*

The stakes are even higher when AI systems are used in governance. China's social credit system exemplifies how algorithmic evaluation can construct identity not as self-expression but as compliance. Citizens are scored based on behaviour, with privileges or restrictions assigned accordingly. In such systems, identity becomes a quantifiable asset, defined less by heritage or individuality than by alignment with the expectations of the state. Contrast this with Western liberal contexts, where algorithms often construct identity through consumer patterns and market segmentation, treating individuals primarily as nodes of economic value. Both cases illustrate that AI mediates identity not in abstract terms but through very concrete forms of recognition, reward, and exclusion.

An important dimension of this debate is the role of memory. Cultural identity is deeply tied to the transmission of stories, rituals, and collective histories. Yet algorithmic systems, driven by the logic of recency and relevance, often privilege the new over the old, the viral over the archival. For example, recommendation engines on video platforms tend to push fresh content to the fore, burying older material regardless of its cultural significance. Over time, this creates a distortion in cultural memory: what is remembered is what algorithms keep visible, while what is forgotten is what the system deems irrelevant to contemporary engagement. In effect, identity becomes future-facing, shaped by a constant churn of novelty, with heritage struggling to find digital oxygen.

The contest over identity in the machine is therefore not a marginal issue but central to the politics of AI. It forces us to ask whether technology will serve as a vessel for cultural continuity or as an engine of erasure and remoulding. The answer, of course, is not predetermined. It depends on design choices, governance frameworks, and the willingness of communities to assert their agency. Projects that embed local traditions into digital tools, policies that mandate representational fairness, and education that foregrounds digital literacy all become crucial arenas in which the struggle over identity is waged.

What is striking, however, is that identity under AI is never static. It is continually negotiated in relation to systems that both constrain and enable, silence and amplify. The encounter between cultural heritage and globalised code is not a one-off collision but an ongoing process of adaptation and resistance. The challenge lies in ensuring that this negotiation remains open rather than predetermined by the invisible logics of datasets and algorithms. *To preserve the richness of human identity in the age of AI is to insist that code serves culture, not the other way around.*

Chapter 8

The New Great Game

For much of the twentieth century, the defining geopolitical contest was framed by nuclear arsenals, oil reserves, and industrial capacity. In the twenty-first, the axis of rivalry has shifted decisively towards artificial intelligence. Whoever masters its development and deployment will shape not only the balance of military power but also the economic hierarchies, cultural flows, and political systems of the coming decades. This competition is not occurring in an abstract technological void; it is structured by values, institutions, and strategic choices. The AI race is not simply about faster processors or larger datasets—it is about who will set the terms of a future order. The two dominant players are unmistakable: the United States and China, each wielding immense resources and divergent political systems that crystallise into contrasting visions of technological governance. This contest is not a sideshow to traditional statecraft; it is the defining rivalry of the century, a struggle over whose model of power and society will be encoded into the digital infrastructures that govern everyday life.

The American strategy has long been rooted in decentralised innovation. Its strength lies in a vast network of private enterprises—Silicon Valley giants, start-ups, research universities—whose entrepreneurial freedom has generated global technological leadership. The United States seeks to maintain this edge through an open ecosystem that attracts talent worldwide, while simultaneously leveraging alliances to set international standards. Yet beneath this story of openness lies a protective instinct: export controls on semiconductors, restrictions on Chinese firms, and a growing determination to weaponise interdependence. For the United States, AI is both a commercial prize and a national security imperative, with its military-industrial complex increasingly entwined with the tech sector.

China, by contrast, embodies a centralised model that fuses state direction with corporate ambition. The Chinese Communist Party has declared

AI a strategic priority, weaving it into its industrial policies, national surveillance infrastructure, and geopolitical outreach through initiatives like the Digital Silk Road. Beijing's advantage lies in scale: vast quantities of data generated by its enormous population, and the political capacity to mobilise entire industries behind national goals. But its ambition goes further than domestic dominance. By exporting surveillance systems, smart city platforms, and AI-enabled infrastructure abroad, China positions itself not merely as a competitor to American technology but as an architect of an alternative technological order. The result is a stark contrast: a liberal-democratic ecosystem that prizes individual freedoms but relies on corporate dominance, against an authoritarian-collectivist model that prioritises state control but promises stability and efficiency.

The global implications of this rivalry extend far beyond Washington and Beijing. Middle powers—nations with significant technological talent but without the financial or infrastructural resources of superpowers—are navigating a delicate strategic terrain. India, for instance, positions itself as a potential third pole, aspiring to harness its demographic dividend and software expertise to avoid permanent dependency on either camp. Yet India's infrastructure gaps and political ambivalence leave it oscillating between opportunities and vulnerabilities. Israel, with its remarkable start-up ecosystem and military-technological synergies, leverages niche expertise—particularly in cybersecurity and defence applications—to punch far above its weight. South Korea, meanwhile, has become a global hub for semiconductor production and consumer technology, balancing an alliance with the United States against the gravitational pull of its Chinese neighbour. These countries exemplify the strategies of hedging and specialisation, carving out influence in niches that allow them to remain relevant despite the shadow of giants.

Yet while middle powers manoeuvre for leverage, vast regions risk being relegated to the periphery of this contest. Africa and Latin America, despite their populations and cultural richness, face the danger of becoming *data colonies*. In such a scenario, their citizens' behaviours, communications, and transactions are mined by foreign platforms, monetised abroad, and used to train AI systems that reflect alien priorities. The infrastructure of digital life—from cloud services to social platforms—is overwhelmingly owned by American or Chinese firms, leaving local actors with little agency in shaping the terms of technological modernity. The danger is not merely economic dependency but cultural erasure, as local contexts are subordinated to foreign algorithms optimised for distant markets.

Some governments have recognised this threat, experimenting with data localisation laws or regional digital alliances, but the asymmetry of resources remains daunting. If Africa and Latin America cannot establish technological sovereignty, they risk being locked into a subordinate position in the emerging global hierarchy.

Beneath these rivalries lies the most profound structural risk of all: the fragmentation of the internet itself. For decades, the promise of the digital sphere was one of universality—an interconnected web linking people across borders. Yet the rise of competing AI standards and regulatory philosophies threatens to splinter this vision into rival internets. Already, there are signs of bifurcation. China has developed a heavily controlled digital ecosystem, shielded by the Great Firewall, which exports its model of cyber-sovereignty to authoritarian allies. The United States and its partners continue to champion a more open internet, yet this too is increasingly subject to geopolitical concerns, as restrictions on data flows, platform access, and AI exports proliferate. The possibility is not a clean division but a patchwork of overlapping digital blocs, each governed by different standards, values, and infrastructures. The consequences of such fragmentation are immense: disruption to global commerce, barriers to cultural exchange, and the erosion of the internet as a shared human commons.

The New Great Game, then, is not simply a metaphor for competition; it is a description of the structural reorganisation of power. Unlike the nineteenth-century contest for territory in Central Asia, today's struggle concerns the invisible architectures of digital life—who controls data, who sets technical standards, who defines the acceptable uses of technology. The stakes are not confined to the geopolitical elite. Every citizen becomes implicated, as their data, identities, and futures are drawn into the orbit of one technological camp or another. The lines of alignment and resistance are being redrawn daily, with choices made in boardrooms, parliaments, and laboratories shaping the contours of a new global order.

To grasp the contours of this struggle is to understand more than a race for technological supremacy. It is to perceive the deep ways in which AI reconfigures international relations, hierarchies of wealth, and cultural legitimacy. The chapter ahead unpacks these dynamics: the fierce rivalry between superpowers, the strategies of middle players seeking room to manoeuvre, the precarious position of regions struggling to escape dependency, and the looming spectre of a fractured internet. Together, these forces reveal a world in which AI is not merely a tool but the primary terrain upon which the future of global order will be decided.

Superpower Rivalries

The defining contest of the twenty-first century is not being fought with tanks, aircraft carriers, or even conventional diplomacy, but through algorithms, data, and the infrastructures of artificial intelligence. For the first time since the Cold War, the world is witnessing two superpowers with the capacity not merely to compete economically and militarily but to shape the very rules of global technological life. The United States and China are locked in a rivalry that will determine who sets the standards of digital governance, who dominates the industries of the future, and whose values are embedded in the code that organises daily existence. Unlike previous contests for power, this struggle does not map neatly onto territory. Instead, it penetrates finance, healthcare, education, defence, and culture, weaving itself into the fibres of human society.

The United States enters this rivalry with historic advantages. It remains home to the most advanced semiconductor design firms, the deepest venture capital ecosystem, and a constellation of technology giants—Google, Microsoft, Meta, Amazon—that not only drive innovation but also shape global digital behaviour. American universities lead in foundational research, while the country continues to attract a disproportionate share of top-tier scientific talent from around the world. These strengths are amplified by the open and competitive nature of its innovation system, in which start-ups can scale rapidly and breakthroughs can be commercialised without excessive bureaucratic interference. Yet this openness is increasingly tempered by strategic caution. Export restrictions on advanced chips, heightened scrutiny of Chinese investment in American firms, and government partnerships with tech companies for military applications reveal how Washington now views AI as an asset too central to national security to be left to market forces alone.

China, meanwhile, has embraced AI as a national project with unmatched intensity. Beijing's 2017 AI development plan set the explicit goal of becoming the world's leading AI power by 2030, mobilising state resources, regulatory authority, and industrial capacity towards this ambition. Where the United States relies on a decentralised private sector, China wields the co-ordination of an authoritarian state, guiding firms like Baidu, Tencent, Alibaba, and Huawei to align their corporate strategies with national priorities. The advantages are considerable: a population generating vast datasets, a political climate tolerant of surveillance, and a state willing to subsidise long-term industrial bets. Chinese advances in facial recognition, natural language processing, and smart city infrastructure demonstrate both technical sophistication and an orientation towards governance applications, reflecting the Party's conviction that AI can serve as a tool of social stability and political control.

The military dimension of this rivalry is profound. The United States retains unmatched global reach, with a network of alliances and bases, but it no longer enjoys unchallenged technological dominance. Both countries view AI as central to the future of warfare—autonomous drones, predictive logistics, cyber operations, and decision-support systems are already reshaping doctrines of combat. Washington has invested in initiatives like the Joint Artificial Intelligence Center to integrate AI across its defence apparatus, while also pursuing partnerships with private firms to ensure technological superiority. China, by contrast, has pursued a doctrine of "intelligentised warfare," envisioning conflicts in which speed of decision-making, enabled by AI systems, outpaces human deliberation. Its investments in swarming drone technologies, hypersonic weapons guided by AI optimisation, and battlefield command systems reflect a belief that the decisive edge will belong to the side that can process information and act upon it fastest. This raises profound ethical and strategic dilemmas: will human judgement be gradually subordinated to algorithmic calculation, and what happens when autonomous systems make lethal mistakes?

Economically, the rivalry reaches into every corner of global trade. AI promises to revolutionise productivity, from manufacturing and logistics to healthcare diagnostics and financial services. The United States champions an ecosystem in which private corporations shape these applications and spread them globally through market dominance. China, by contrast, pursues a model of state-guided diffusion, tying AI development to industrial upgrading under its "Made in China 2025" strategy. This has already altered supply chains: Western firms rely heavily on Chinese manufacturing capacity, while Chinese firms remain dependent on American-designed chips and software ecosystems. Each side is acutely aware of its vulnerabilities, fuelling efforts at "decoupling" or "de-risking." The American CHIPS and Science Act, with its subsidies for domestic semiconductor production, mirrors Chinese investments in self-sufficiency. The outcome of this race for technological independence will determine not only bilateral relations but also the global distribution of economic power for decades.

The rivalry also carries profound cultural dimensions. AI is not a neutral tool; it encodes assumptions about privacy, authority, fairness, and efficiency. American systems, even when built by corporations, generally reflect liberal values of individual choice and market competition—albeit filtered through the commercial logic of profit and data extraction. Chinese systems, by contrast, often reflect collectivist values, embedding mechanisms of social control and aligning technological systems with state objectives. When exported abroad, these differences matter. Surveillance platforms built by Chinese firms have been deployed across Africa, Latin America, and parts of Europe, bringing with them implicit models of governance. American platforms dominate global search, social networking, and e-commerce, exporting both cultural products and behavioural norms. Thus, the rivalry is not only about economics or warfighting capacity but about whose model of society becomes the de facto template for billions of lives.

Neither superpower faces a straightforward path to dominance. The United States must balance its entrepreneurial culture with mounting political polarisation, regulatory uncertainty, and challenges in integrating cutting-edge AI into public institutions. China, for its part, must contend with slowing economic growth, demographic pressures, and the risks inherent in a top-down innovation system that can sometimes stifle the very creativity it seeks to harness. Moreover, both countries face the challenge of global perception. Allies and partners, from Europe to Southeast Asia, are wary of overdependence on either side. The European Union, for example, is attempting to chart a middle course by regulating AI according to its own normative frameworks, emphasising human rights and ethical governance. This creates a multipolar contest, in which superpower rivalry intersects with regional assertions of autonomy.

The U.S.–China rivalry in AI is thus more than a bilateral contest. It is the central axis of a global struggle over power, prosperity, and legitimacy. The technologies being developed will not only shape the fortunes of these two states but will reorder the structures of global society—how wars are fought, how economies grow, how citizens live and interact. The rivalry's outcome is not predetermined. It will be shaped by policy decisions, technological breakthroughs, cultural choices, and the unpredictable feedback loops of innovation itself. What is clear is that the stakes are nothing less than the future configuration of world order. AI has become the terrain on which the most powerful states in history are testing their strength, and the rest of the world must reckon with the consequences.

Middle Powers and Their Strategies

Global narratives of technological rivalry often portray the world as a binary struggle between the United States and China. Yet such framing misses a crucial reality: *the map of AI power is also being redrawn by middle powers*—nations without the colossal resources of the superpowers but with sufficient capacity, strategic acumen, and cultural capital to shape the contours of the future. These countries do not simply accept their fate as passive spectators. Instead, they carve out niches, cultivate alliances, and build ecosystems that allow them to exert influence disproportionate to their size. Their efforts highlight an important truth: in the emerging AI order, agency is not monopolised by giants.

India, Israel, and South Korea stand out as compelling case studies of this dynamic. Each faces structural constraints—be it capital, scale, or dependence on foreign technologies—that would appear to limit its ability to compete with the superpowers. Yet each has developed strategies tailored to its unique strengths, creating openings to assert influence. Collectively, these strategies illuminate how states in the middle tier can reframe their vulnerabilities as assets, finding leverage in agility, regional leadership, or specialisation.

India presents the most complex case. With its 1.4 billion people and vast digital infrastructure, it possesses raw scale that places it closer to the category of a civilisational state than a traditional middle power. Yet in technological terms, it faces the persistent dilemma of dependence: advanced semiconductors, leading-edge hardware, and proprietary AI models remain largely outside its control. Recognising this, New Delhi has pursued a dual-track strategy. Domestically, it leverages its human capital—the world's largest pool of software engineers and IT professionals—while building digital public goods at unprecedented scale. Initiatives such as Aadhaar, the biometric identity system, and the Unified Payments Interface have not only transformed governance and commerce at home but also provided India with models of digital infrastructure that other countries now look to emulate. Internationally, India has positioned itself as a voice of the Global South, advocating for data sovereignty and more equitable distribution of AI benefits. By doing so, it turns its vulnerability—the risk of being a data colony—into a platform for leadership, arguing that digital governance must not become another domain of great-power dominance. The challenge lies in whether India can translate its software strengths into breakthroughs in hardware and fundamental research, areas where its dependence remains acute.

Israel's approach is strikingly different, shaped by its geopolitical isolation and acute security environment. Lacking the sheer scale of population or markets, Israel has turned necessity into advantage by cultivating an innovation ecosystem oriented towards agility, defence, and niche expertise. Its military, particularly the fabled Unit 8200, has been a crucible of technological talent, seeding a start-up culture that prizes rapid iteration and applied solutions. This has enabled Israel to become a global hub for cybersecurity and AI applications in defence, surveillance, and fintech. Israeli firms, often backed by foreign venture capital and seeking global markets from the outset, punch far above their weight. Yet the country's reliance on external partners for scaling and its exposure to geopolitical pressures mean its influence is often exercised indirectly, through technologies embedded in global supply chains or acquired by multinational giants. Israel's success underscores an important lesson: middle powers can wield influence not by competing across the entire AI spectrum but by mastering select domains where their expertise is indispensable.

South Korea illustrates yet another model, one grounded in industrial policy and cultural projection. Having long been a "fast follower" in technology, Seoul has in recent decades cultivated global champions such as Samsung and LG, whose role in semiconductors and electronics makes South Korea central to the AI hardware ecosystem. Unlike Israel, South Korea possesses both scale and industrial muscle, yet it lacks the hegemonic ambition of a superpower. Instead, it has pursued influence through supply-chain indispensability and cultural soft power. The former ensures that no conversation about semiconductors—arguably the most critical chokepoint in AI development—can ignore South Korea. The latter, epitomised by the global spread of K-pop, Korean cinema, and digital gaming, positions South Korea not only as a hardware provider but as a cultural shaper of digital identities. This dual leverage—hard technological capacity and soft cultural influence—offers a unique model of how a middle power can remain indispensable to both East and West without committing entirely to one side of the rivalry.

These three cases illustrate divergent strategies, yet common threads run through them. First, middle powers often succeed not by trying to replicate the superpowers' breadth but by specialising. India leverages human capital and digital public infrastructure; Israel thrives on defence-driven innovation; South Korea capitalises on industrial capacity and cultural projection. Second, each recognises that autonomy is relative.

Total independence from the superpowers is illusory; instead, the goal is to maximise bargaining power by ensuring indispensability in particular niches. Third, these states understand that narratives matter. India's championing of digital sovereignty, Israel's portrayal of itself as a security innovator, and South Korea's global cultural presence all shape international perceptions and, by extension, their influence.

Tensions, however, complicate these strategies. India's ambition to lead the Global South is undermined by its reliance on Western and Chinese technologies, creating a delicate balancing act between cooperation and autonomy. Israel's deep integration with U.S. technology ecosystems strengthens its capabilities but exposes it to shifts in American politics and global norms on surveillance and warfare. South Korea's indispensability in semiconductors is both an asset and a vulnerability, as it finds itself under pressure from both Washington and Beijing to align with their competing visions of supply chain security. For all three, the risk lies in overdependence on external actors even as they seek to project independence.

Philosophically, the strategies of middle powers highlight a more general principle about power in the algorithmic age: *influence is no longer strictly a function of size.* Just as start-ups can disrupt incumbents with focused innovation, states without hegemonic resources can matter disproportionately if they identify the right levers. This does not diminish the dominance of the United States and China, but it complicates the narrative of inevitability. A world shaped only by superpower rivalry overlooks the diverse experiments and innovations emerging from the middle tier. These experiments are not marginal. They set precedents, shape norms, and sometimes create entirely new paths that even the superpowers must follow.

It would be a mistake to view these strategies as static. As AI technologies evolve, so too will the calculus of middle powers. India's vast domestic market may allow it to incubate AI applications suited to the Global South, positioning it as a model provider for other emerging economies. Israel's expertise in edge technologies like quantum computing or medical AI could give it fresh avenues of influence beyond defence. South Korea's continuing bet on both hardware and cultural exports might allow it to extend its dual leverage into the AI era in ways not yet fully visible. What unites them is not a particular outcome but a mindset: that relevance is created, not inherited, and that agency remains possible even in a world of giants.

For observers, the rise of these middle-power strategies carries a sobering implication. The story of AI geopolitics is not reducible to a bipolar contest. Rather, it is a layered game in which states of different sizes and capacities pursue influence according to their own logics. Recognising this complexity is essential to understanding the future. For beneath the clash of superpowers lies a more nuanced struggle—one in which nations like India, Israel, and South Korea quietly redraw the rules of engagement, proving that even without superpower resources, there are ways to matter in the empire of algorithms.

The Forgotten South

The world's most valuable resource is no longer oil, but data. Yet for much of Africa and Latin America, the extraction of this new wealth increasingly resembles the extractive economies of the colonial past: raw material leaves the continent, refined value accrues elsewhere, and the societies from which it was drawn remain peripheral to the centres of power. The difference is that the resource in question is not gold or rubber but the digital traces of billions of people—search histories, biometric identifiers, purchasing behaviours, and the myriad signals generated by smartphones and sensors. The danger is not simply economic dependency but the deeper risk of *data colonialism*: an arrangement in which these regions are locked into permanent subordination, feeding the global AI system without shaping its design, standards, or benefits.

Africa's position illustrates the paradox starkly. On one hand, it is the fastest-growing digital market in the world, with mobile adoption soaring, internet penetration deepening, and youthful demographics generating an unparalleled flow of behavioural data. On the other, it remains structurally dependent on infrastructure and platforms controlled elsewhere. The vast majority of data centres are located outside the continent, forcing African states to rely on foreign providers for storage, cloud services, and computational power. This creates both latency and vulnerability: a continent generating data at scale must send it abroad for processing, often under terms that favour the corporations and governments hosting those centres. Efforts to reverse this pattern—such as Kenya's Konza Technopolis or South Africa's attempts to expand local cloud capacity—have gained traction but remain modest in comparison to the global giants. The asymmetry persists: Africa is producing the fuel for AI systems but capturing only a sliver of the value.

Latin America's trajectory is similarly double-edged. With strong urbanisation, widespread smartphone adoption, and diverse economies, it is a region rich in data flows. Brazil in particular has emerged as a leader in digital governance with its General Data Protection Law (LGPD), signalling a desire to assert sovereignty over data. Yet even here, dependency remains acute. Major AI research centres, cloud infrastructure, and venture capital remain concentrated in North America, Europe, and increasingly China. Latin American platforms and applications, even when homegrown, often run on foreign-owned systems. This structural imbalance leaves the region vulnerable to exploitation and limits its ability to set terms in the global AI order. The effect is a deepening of the very patterns of dependency that economic theorists in the twentieth century identified under dependency theory: the centre innovates and governs, while the periphery provides inputs and consumes finished products.

This structural imbalance raises profound cultural questions. The datasets used to train AI models are disproportionately sourced from Western contexts or shaped by Western epistemologies. As these systems spread into Africa and Latin America, they risk entrenching cultural erasures. Voice recognition systems often fail with African accents; predictive algorithms designed for North American healthcare settings may misdiagnose or mis-prioritise patients in Brazilian favelas. When the tools shaping governance, education, and commerce are trained primarily on foreign datasets, *local cultures become invisible in the algorithmic imagination*. This invisibility has consequences: it shapes whose values are prioritised, whose languages are encoded, and whose histories are recognised.

Resistance is not absent. Across Africa, the idea of "data sovereignty" has gained ground, with governments recognising that allowing unregulated data extraction is equivalent to conceding long-term control over economic futures. The African Union has begun advancing a continental framework for data governance, seeking to harmonise standards and build capacity. Countries such as Nigeria and Rwanda are experimenting with local AI strategies, aiming to nurture domestic research ecosystems. Latin America, meanwhile, has seen increasing regional dialogue, with Brazil, Chile, and Mexico attempting to coordinate around digital rights and infrastructure investment. These efforts, however, face immense challenges: limited capital, talent migration, and political instability often undercut ambitious plans.

The broader question is whether Africa and Latin America can leapfrog into meaningful participation in the AI order, or whether they will be confined to subordinate roles. Advocates of leapfrogging argue that just as mobile phones allowed African societies to bypass landline infrastructure, so too might cloud computing or open-source AI models allow local innovators to circumvent dependence on superpower platforms. The rise of AI research hubs in places like Accra and São Paulo points to this possibility. Yet critics caution that leapfrogging narratives often underestimate the entrenched power of global supply chains. Unlike mobile telephony, AI depends heavily on hardware—semiconductors, GPUs, data centres—that require vast capital investments and are dominated by a handful of global players. Without addressing this material infrastructure gap, leapfrogging risks becoming more aspiration than reality.

The economic consequences of being reduced to a data colony are sobering. Value accrues not at the point of data generation but at the point of refinement—where machine learning models are trained, deployed, and monetised. If Africa and Latin America remain mere suppliers of raw data, they risk replaying the resource-curse dynamics of the past: exporting raw commodities while importing finished products at higher costs. The result is not simply lost revenue but lost sovereignty, as critical sectors such as healthcare, education, and finance become dependent on foreign-owned systems. The irony is acute: regions rich in human potential, cultural diversity, and untapped markets may find themselves locked into a cycle where their very participation in the digital economy deepens dependency.

There is also a geopolitical dimension. Both the United States and China view Africa and Latin America as arenas of competition, offering infrastructure investments, cloud services, and AI partnerships. For Washington, initiatives like the U.S.-Africa Leaders Summit and investments by tech giants such as Microsoft and Google are attempts to counter China's digital Belt and Road strategy, which has brought Huawei networks and Chinese data centres to dozens of African countries. Latin America faces similar dynamics, with Chinese firms investing heavily in smart cities and surveillance infrastructure from Ecuador to Argentina. While these partnerships can bring immediate benefits—connectivity, capital, and access to technology—they also risk entrenching long-term dependency, as local governments lock themselves into ecosystems designed elsewhere.

Philosophically, the struggle of the Global South reveals a deeper tension about the nature of digital modernity. Is participation in the global AI system inherently a form of dependency, or can regions like Africa and Latin America shape its trajectory in their own image? Advocates of digital sovereignty insist on the latter, arguing that *true modernity requires the ability not just to consume algorithms but to write them.* Yet this aspiration collides with structural realities: brain drain siphons off talent to Silicon Valley or Shenzhen, while capital constraints limit the scaling of local innovation. The result is a constant tension between ambition and constraint, sovereignty and dependency.

What is clear is that the stakes extend beyond economics. The question of whether Africa and Latin America become permanent data colonies is also a question about cultural identity, political autonomy, and global justice. If the future of AI is written overwhelmingly by the North, the South risks being relegated not just to the margins of the economy but to the margins of history itself. Conversely, if these regions succeed in asserting agency—through coordinated governance, local innovation, and strategic alliances—they may not only escape dependency but contribute unique perspectives that enrich the global AI order. For in their struggles lies the possibility of redefining modernity itself, demonstrating that technological futures need not be monopolised by giants but can also be shaped from the periphery.

The Risk of Splintered Internets

The promise of the internet was once its universality: a single, open network where information could flow freely across borders, cultures, and markets. That vision is increasingly under strain. The rise of artificial intelligence has introduced not only new capabilities but also new fault lines, and there is growing evidence that the internet may fracture into competing domains governed by divergent AI standards, regulatory regimes, and political ideologies. What was imagined as a borderless commons may give way to a world of segmented digital sovereignties, where access, content, and even algorithms are shaped by the rivalries of states and blocs. The central question is whether humanity is moving towards one internet or many, and whether fragmentation is a temporary phase of adaptation or the new structural condition of digital life.

The roots of this splintering lie partly in geopolitics. The United States and China, the two leading AI powers, approach digital governance from profoundly different premises. Washington, despite its ambivalence over regulation, tends to emphasise individual rights, market-driven innovation, and alliances that preserve open flows of information—though this openness is bounded by national security concerns. Beijing, by contrast, integrates AI development into its centralised model of governance, linking data, surveillance, and strategic industrial policy. Its standards emphasise state control, prioritising social stability and political legitimacy over unrestrained openness. As both models diffuse globally—through cloud platforms, telecoms infrastructure, and AI-driven applications—they pull countries into competing spheres of technical and political alignment. The internet becomes less a neutral conduit and more a contested terrain where competing AI philosophies are embedded in code.

The risk of fragmentation is not theoretical; it is already visible. China's Great Firewall, once dismissed as an anomaly, has become a template for other states seeking to assert digital sovereignty. Russia has built its own tightly controlled Runet, capable of decoupling from global networks. In India, debates around data localisation and the banning of Chinese apps point to an emerging model of selective openness. Meanwhile, in Europe, the General Data Protection Regulation (GDPR) has effectively set global privacy standards by exporting compliance requirements beyond its borders, while its forthcoming AI Act is poised to shape the terms of algorithmic accountability worldwide. Each of these frameworks is rational on its own terms, yet collectively they risk creating incompatible rulesets. An AI system compliant in Brussels may not be legal in Beijing; a dataset usable in California may be restricted in São Paulo. The effect is an internet no longer defined by universal protocols but by regional architectures of trust, law, and control.

The consequences extend beyond governance to the core architecture of AI. Algorithms are not neutral; they encode the values and priorities of their creators. In a fragmented internet, AI systems will increasingly diverge not only in capability but in orientation. A content recommendation engine designed under European standards of human dignity and anti-discrimination may function very differently from one trained under Chinese imperatives of social harmony and political stability. The divergence is not merely technical but civilisational, reflecting deeper disagreements about the purpose of technology in society. If this trajectory persists, users in different parts of the world will experience fundamentally different versions of the digital sphere, each curated and constrained by the AI standards of their governing bloc.

Supporters of fragmentation argue that it is not inherently destructive. Just as nations regulate financial systems, borders, and media to reflect their values, so too might they regulate AI to preserve sovereignty. From this perspective, the splintering of the internet is a natural correction, ensuring that digital life reflects pluralism rather than a homogenising universalism. In Africa and Latin America, some policymakers view fragmentation as an opportunity to assert control over data flows, protecting local interests against domination by Silicon Valley or Shenzhen. In this reading, a multipolar digital world might empower middle powers and regions of the Global South to carve out their own digital destinies rather than submit to a one-size-fits-all internet.

Yet critics warn that fragmentation comes with steep costs. The internet's power has always rested on network effects—the more people connected, the greater the value for all. A bifurcated or fractured system undermines this by erecting barriers that stifle innovation, limit collaboration, and complicate global commerce. For multinational businesses, divergent AI standards threaten to increase compliance costs and slow deployment. For researchers, data silos weaken the quality of AI training sets, as models lose access to the global diversity of languages, cultures, and contexts. For ordinary citizens, fragmentation risks exacerbating inequality: those in wealthy regions may access advanced AI ecosystems, while those in isolated networks may be confined to inferior tools. The splintering of the internet, in short, threatens to erode the very universality that made it transformative.

There is also the danger of escalation. Once digital standards become proxies for geopolitical rivalry, the internet risks hardening into blocs akin to Cold War alliances. A country adopting Huawei's infrastructure may find itself bound into China's AI ecosystem, while one aligning with U.S. platforms becomes dependent on Silicon Valley's rules and surveillance alliances. Neutrality becomes difficult, as technical interoperability is shaped by political loyalty. The possibility of a "digital Iron Curtain" looms, with countries forced to choose sides in an AI-driven order. The long-term outcome is not only fragmented connectivity but a deepening of global divisions, as the internet ceases to be a space of dialogue and becomes instead a mirror of geopolitical confrontation.

The paradox is that while fragmentation appears likely, there remain powerful incentives for cooperation. Global commerce depends on interoperability; scientific progress thrives on shared data; even national security benefits from certain forms of collaboration. The challenge is to reconcile these universal needs with divergent political values. Institutions like the International Telecommunication Union (ITU) and new initiatives around AI governance seek to establish common frameworks, yet their authority is limited and often contested. The real test will be whether states can find ways to preserve a baseline of shared standards—technical protocols, cybersecurity norms, cross-border data agreements—while allowing for diversity in higher-order governance. Without such efforts, the centrifugal forces of geopolitics may overwhelm the centripetal pull of global interdependence.

Ultimately, the risk of splintered internets raises a deeper question about the nature of the digital order. Is the internet to be understood as a global commons, requiring stewardship for the benefit of all, or as a domain of sovereignty, to be carved into national and regional jurisdictions? The answer will not be uniform, but the balance struck will shape the character of AI's integration into human society. A fractured internet may preserve political autonomy but at the cost of shared progress; a unified internet may foster innovation but risk domination by the most powerful players. The debate is not only technical but philosophical, touching on what humanity values more: sovereignty or universality, pluralism or interoperability.

What is at stake is not simply the shape of the internet but the trajectory of global power. If AI is the defining technology of the century, then the standards governing its use will determine the contours of international order. Whether the internet remains whole or fragments into pieces will decide not just how algorithms function but how nations interact, how cultures communicate, and how knowledge itself circulates. It is a decision being made incrementally—through regulations, investments, alliances, and infrastructure—and its consequences will be felt long after the immediate rivalries have passed. The risk is real, but so too is the possibility of a more balanced digital order, provided the choices made today are informed by both the lessons of history and the urgency of the present.

Chapter 9

Human Agency at the Edge of Empire

The question of human freedom has never been abstract. It has always been shaped by the institutions, technologies, and structures of power through which societies organise themselves. In earlier centuries, the debate centred on monarchs and parliaments, markets and empires, revolutions and reforms. Today, the contours of the debate are shifting. Algorithms now sit in the spaces once occupied by clerks, advisors, and even legislators. They write the rules of our attention, nudge our habits of consumption, and increasingly advise on decisions of law, medicine, and war. What emerges is not a sudden collapse of human freedom, but a gradual narrowing of the circle in which choice operates, a phenomenon made all the more insidious because it often appears as convenience. The future of agency is being reshaped not through overt coercion but through defaults, automation, and systems that quietly embed assumptions into the fabric of daily life.

Consider the act of choosing what to read. Once a decision shaped by libraries, newspapers, or booksellers, it is now filtered by recommendation systems, whose invisible logic defines the menu before us. In health care, diagnostic algorithms trained on vast datasets can suggest treatments more accurately than many clinicians. Yet each suggestion is accompanied by a subtle displacement of authority: does the patient consent to the doctor's advice, or to the machine's? In political discourse, feeds are curated not by editorial boards but by predictive models optimised for engagement. To opt out of these systems is increasingly impractical, if not impossible. The individual remains free in theory, yet the shape of that freedom is quietly channelled, narrowed, and predetermined. *The shrinking circle of choice is not announced with fanfare; it is experienced as an incremental erosion, the gradual surrender of agency under the guise of efficiency.*

This transformation raises profound dilemmas for citizenship. If national destinies are increasingly coded into algorithms—shaping security doctrines, allocating welfare, predicting unrest—what becomes of the citizen's role in a democracy? The traditional story of politics rests on deliberation, accountability, and the idea that the people, through their representatives, make collective decisions. But what happens when those decisions are outsourced to predictive models? A citizen may cast a vote, yet the policies that shape their future are increasingly informed by systems they neither understand nor control. Transparency remains elusive: machine learning models operate as black boxes, and even their creators often struggle to explain their reasoning. Accountability, too, becomes slippery: if an algorithm denies a loan or misclassifies a protest, is the fault the data scientist's, the policymaker's, or the machine's? The citizen is left not only disempowered but also disoriented, caught in a system where political agency becomes decoupled from technological authority.

Yet resignation is not inevitable. Across the world, spaces of resistance are emerging, where activists, technologists, and policymakers seek to keep human values in the loop. The debates over facial recognition in cities such as San Francisco or London demonstrate that societies can push back against surveillance regimes, even when those regimes claim efficiency and safety as their justification. Grassroots movements have campaigned successfully for moratoria, demanding that the deployment of AI systems be matched by democratic oversight. In the European Union, the forthcoming AI Act reflects an attempt to embed human dignity into law, categorising certain uses of AI as "high risk" and placing explicit requirements for accountability. In India, civil society organisations have challenged opaque welfare algorithms that excluded vulnerable populations from basic services, reframing technical debates as questions of justice. These efforts may appear fragmented, but they reveal a deeper pattern: *human agency can be defended not only through individual acts of resistance but through collective insistence that technology remain accountable to human values.*

The struggle to reclaim agency must also extend beyond resistance into political imagination. It is not enough to critique algorithms or demand transparency in narrow cases; citizens must insist that the deployment of AI itself remain subject to political will, rather than being treated as a technical inevitability. This requires reframing the conversation: AI is not a neutral tool but a site of power, where choices about data, models, and applications embed visions of society. Should predictive policing be banned altogether, or merely monitored? Should algorithmic scoring of credit or insurance be limited to narrow categories, or abolished as unjust by design? Should autonomous weapons be outlawed, regardless of their tactical utility? These are not engineering questions; they are political ones, requiring public debate, legislation, and collective decision-making. The danger is that without such engagement, the terms of the future will be set not by citizens but by corporations and governments, each pursuing their interests while framing technological deployment as inevitable progress.

The chapter ahead argues that the stakes could not be higher. If the circle of choice continues to shrink unchecked, human agency risks becoming a vestige—preserved in rhetoric but hollow in practice. If the citizen's dilemma is ignored, democracy itself may be reconfigured into a managerial system where algorithms anticipate needs and neutralise dissent. But the emergence of spaces of resistance signals that alternative trajectories remain possible, provided societies are willing to confront the hard questions of power, accountability, and human oversight. Ultimately, the challenge is not merely to adapt to AI but to reclaim the political, ensuring that the empire of algorithms does not render citizens passive subjects but active agents in shaping their collective destiny.

This chapter explores precisely that tension: how individuals and societies navigate the narrowing avenues of choice, how moral responsibility is redefined under algorithmic governance, and how resistance can be translated into institutional reforms. It does not promise easy solutions. But it does insist that the question of agency remains urgent, and that the answers we provide will determine not only the balance of power between humans and machines but also the character of the societies we inhabit. For in the end, the edge of empire is not a distant frontier; it is the space in which each citizen decides whether to cede their voice to the machine or to demand that their voice still matters.

The Shrinking Circle of Choice

Freedom often reveals itself not in grand gestures but in the smallest decisions of daily life. What to read, what to watch, what route to take to work, which loan to apply for, whom to connect with—all appear trivial in isolation but collectively form the texture of individual autonomy. The paradox of our technological age is that just as these choices proliferate in theory, their practical scope is increasingly narrowed by systems that pre-select, prioritise, and personalise. The proliferation of algorithmic defaults means that fewer decisions are made consciously by individuals, and more are silently shaped in advance by statistical models optimised for efficiency, profit, or control. *The circle of human choice is not eradicated outright; it is compressed to the edges, leaving us to operate within boundaries drawn by machines we did not design and cannot easily interrogate.*

The experience is familiar to anyone who has opened a streaming platform. Instead of browsing an entire catalogue, users are presented with curated lists that claim to "understand" their preferences. Netflix, for instance, maintains not one homepage but thousands, each personalised according to predicted behaviour. The recommendation engine becomes not a supplement but the default route into content, to the point where a large share of what is watched originates from algorithmic nudges rather than deliberate search. This dynamic extends far beyond entertainment. In finance, credit-scoring systems decide eligibility before human interaction occurs, effectively eliminating the very possibility of negotiation for millions. In healthcare, diagnostic tools advise clinicians in ways that create strong pressure to defer to the machine, especially when liability fears loom large. In politics, algorithmic feeds distribute information with a precision that reshapes public discourse. What is striking is not only the ubiquity of these systems but the subtlety with which they recast agency. *We still choose, but from a menu that has already been written for us.*

It is tempting to interpret this narrowing as benign or even beneficial. After all, who mourns the loss of endless scrolling when a system can deliver what we "want" with uncanny accuracy? Who resists a navigation app that steers them efficiently through traffic? The seduction of convenience masks the deeper structural shift. Defaults, once chosen for simplicity, become powerful determinants of behaviour. Research in behavioural economics demonstrates how sticky defaults are: from pension enrolment to organ donation, the majority of individuals accept the pre-set option, not out of agreement but out of inertia. When algorithms become the architects of defaults at scale, their ability to shape collective outcomes surpasses even the most paternalistic bureaucracies of the past. Unlike a civil servant drafting regulations, the algorithm operates invisibly, updating constantly, and learning from feedback in ways opaque to those subject to its influence.

The implications reach into the moral and political core of agency. A citizen's power is traditionally exercised through deliberation and choice. Yet deliberation requires exposure to alternatives, and choice requires an open field in which to decide. As algorithms progressively narrow what we see, recommend what we should buy, and predict what we are likely to do, the preconditions for meaningful choice erode. Consider electoral politics. In many democracies, campaigns are now micro-targeted, with citizens shown not the same manifestos but individually tailored appeals generated by predictive models. The public sphere fragments into overlapping but divergent information environments, leaving citizens less like participants in a shared debate and more like subjects in parallel experiments. The vote remains, but the path to that vote is subtly conditioned, and the sense of collective deliberation—on which democracy depends—is weakened.

Critics might argue that human beings have always navigated environments structured by defaults. Newspapers have long decided which stories to put on the front page, supermarkets which products to display at eye level. Yet the analogy only goes so far. What distinguishes algorithmic systems is their scalability, speed, and adaptiveness. The newspaper editor made a finite number of choices each day, open to scrutiny and critique. The algorithm recalibrates constantly, shaping millions of micro-decisions in real time, while its logic remains inaccessible. The supermarket's arrangement of products can be resisted by deliberate shoppers; an algorithmically ranked search result is far harder to escape. The difference is one of magnitude and opacity: traditional defaults were visible and contestable, whereas algorithmic defaults are dynamic, personalised, and largely inscrutable. *What appears to be more freedom of choice is in fact a deeper dependency on systems that quietly configure the boundaries of that choice.*

This narrowing also has uneven effects, accentuating social inequalities. Defaults designed on the basis of historical data risk reproducing existing biases. In welfare distribution, algorithmic systems have denied benefits to vulnerable populations because the data encoded assumptions about who was "deserving." In predictive policing, models trained on skewed datasets direct officers disproportionately to minority neighbourhoods, reinforcing cycles of surveillance and suspicion. For those with resources and expertise, there remain workarounds—lawyers to contest algorithmic decisions, private platforms to bypass mainstream feeds. For the less privileged, the defaults become binding, their choices truncated not by explicit prohibition but by invisible barriers embedded in code. Here, the shrinking circle of choice is not merely a philosophical concern; it is a matter of justice.

Yet the erosion of agency is not irreversible. Awareness itself is a form of resistance. When cities debate bans on facial recognition, or regulators demand explainability in credit algorithms, they are asserting that defaults must be accountable to the public, not just to technical accuracy. In design circles, there is a growing emphasis on "human-centred AI," which seeks to build systems that augment rather than replace decision-making. While such initiatives are often criticised as aspirational, they signal an important shift: that the politics of AI lies not only in outcomes but in the architecture of choice itself. Defaults can be designed to empower rather than constrain, to expand the sphere of agency rather than compress it. But this requires conscious political will, not the passive acceptance of whatever configuration corporations or governments deem most efficient.

The shrinking circle of choice is not simply a technological phenomenon but a cultural and political one. It reflects how societies balance the desire for convenience against the value of autonomy, how they negotiate the tension between efficiency and freedom. At its heart lies a question that is as much moral as technical: do we want to live in a world where our paths are subtly guided by systems that predict us better than we know ourselves, or do we insist on preserving the space for surprise, deliberation, and dissent? The answer cannot be left to engineers alone. It requires public deliberation, democratic institutions, and a renewed insistence that the defaults shaping our lives be open to contestation. For the circle of choice will shrink only as far as societies allow it to—and its preservation, or restoration, is a matter of collective decision rather than technical inevitability.

The narrowing of human agency under algorithmic defaults is thus a defining challenge of our age. It forces us to confront the trade-offs between autonomy and efficiency, between predictability and freedom. It invites us to reconsider the very meaning of choice in a world where every decision is prefigured by models trained on our past. To ignore this dynamic is to accept a quiet surrender of autonomy; to confront it is to reclaim the possibility that technology can serve human freedom rather than constrict it. What hangs in the balance is not only the scope of individual decisions but the texture of citizenship, democracy, and the moral life itself.

The Citizen's Dilemma

Few forces in history have determined the trajectory of nations as profoundly as the capacity to encode rules, whether in constitutions, bureaucratic procedures, or financial systems. What distinguishes our moment is that many of those rules are now being written not in parliamentary halls but in the hidden logic of algorithms. National destinies—once argued over in public squares and legislative chambers—are increasingly shaped by the weight of machine-driven calculations. From the allocation of welfare to the management of borders, from the steering of economic investments to the prioritisation of military threats, artificial intelligence has become a new kind of lawgiver. The citizen finds themselves in a paradoxical position: formally free, yet bound by decisions whose rationale is often inaccessible.

The dilemma lies in reconciling the democratic promise of individual agency with the opaque determinism of machine-coded governance.

Nowhere is this tension more visible than in social welfare systems. In the Netherlands, the SyRI programme was designed to detect welfare fraud by cross-referencing vast amounts of personal data. Citizens flagged by the system faced punitive scrutiny, yet were never told how the algorithm arrived at its suspicion. After years of controversy, the Dutch courts ruled the system violated human rights principles, particularly the right to privacy and due process. For ordinary people, the experience was not only of bureaucratic overreach but of disenfranchisement: their fates were dictated by a system they could neither question nor understand. This episode captures the crux of the dilemma. A democracy that encodes national policy into unaccountable algorithms risks hollowing out the very notion of citizenship, replacing participation with passive compliance.

The difficulty intensifies when AI is applied to security and migration. Consider the European Union's growing reliance on predictive analytics to manage its borders. Systems estimate the likelihood of asylum claims being "legitimate" or predict potential unrest in countries of origin, thereby guiding decisions that affect thousands of lives. These predictions are not neutral; they are the product of models trained on historical patterns that inevitably encode bias. A refugee fleeing a novel form of persecution may find their case undermined because it does not fit the statistical mould of past claims. For the citizen observing such practices, the dilemma is profound. On the one hand, the state has a legitimate interest in managing flows and maintaining security. On the other, the individual conscience recoils at the idea of human beings reduced to data points in probabilistic equations. *The question is no longer simply about rights within the nation, but about the moral legitimacy of national decisions when mediated by machine intelligence.*

One response has been to argue for a redefinition of citizenship in the digital age. Rather than being confined to voting and formal participation, citizenship must include the right to demand algorithmic accountability. The European Union's General Data Protection Regulation (GDPR), with its provisions for the right to explanation, represents a tentative step in this direction. Yet in practice, explanations are often couched in technical jargon that neither clarifies nor empowers. The real issue is not whether an algorithm can be explained in principle, but whether citizens are given meaningful avenues to contest and shape the rules encoded within them. Without this, the promise of transparency becomes a bureaucratic fig leaf.

True agency requires not just information but the capacity to influence the systems that govern one's life.

Critics counter that such demands are unrealistic. The complexity of modern AI systems is such that even their designers struggle to explain their outputs in human-readable terms. If governance is to benefit from the predictive power of these tools, some argue, citizens must accept a trade-off: less transparency in exchange for greater efficiency and accuracy. This argument, however, risks reintroducing a technocratic paternalism under the guise of objectivity. Efficiency is not a self-justifying value in politics; it must always be weighed against principles of justice, fairness, and consent. A society that prioritises algorithmic accuracy over democratic deliberation is not merely more efficient—it is differently governed, with sovereignty displaced from citizens to systems.

The dilemma is sharpened by the geopolitical stakes. National adoption of AI is often justified in terms of global competition. Governments argue that to slow down in the pursuit of accountability is to cede strategic ground to rivals less concerned with rights and freedoms. China's model of digital governance—combining AI surveillance with centralised political control—looms as both a warning and an implicit benchmark. Western democracies face the temptation to quietly emulate aspects of this model under the pressure of security and competitiveness, while maintaining a rhetorical commitment to freedom. For the citizen, the dilemma becomes existential: how to defend democratic agency in an age where even democracies appear willing to trade it away under the logic of technological necessity.

Yet citizens are not powerless. Around the world, movements have emerged that challenge the unchecked use of AI in governance. In the United States, campaigns have succeeded in banning predictive policing tools in cities such as Oakland and Santa Cruz, citing their discriminatory effects. In India, activists have resisted the expansion of the Aadhaar biometric identity system into areas of welfare distribution where errors could prove fatal for the poorest. These struggles illustrate that agency persists when citizens organise to demand accountability. They also highlight the need for new forms of political literacy. Just as the industrial revolution required citizens to grapple with the social consequences of mechanisation, the algorithmic age demands a citizenry capable of engaging with questions of data, bias, and design. *Political agency in the twenty-first century cannot be exercised without a basic fluency in the technologies that increasingly define governance.*

There remains, however, a philosophical unease. If machines can predict human behaviour with increasing accuracy, is agency itself diminished? Are citizens truly free if their decisions can be modelled and nudged by systems that exploit cognitive biases? Some philosophers argue that agency has always been exercised within constraints—social, economic, cultural. Algorithms are but the latest in a long line of influences. The difference, however, lies in scale and intentionality. Whereas cultural norms evolve organically, algorithms are designed to steer outcomes with precision, often in service of commercial or political goals. The citizen's dilemma is not whether to accept influence—no human choice is free from it—but whether to tolerate systems designed to exploit influence systematically and invisibly.

The challenge, then, is to carve out *spaces of resistance* where citizens can insist upon their role not as subjects of algorithmic governance but as shapers of it. This might involve legal frameworks that enshrine rights to contest algorithmic decisions, educational programmes that build digital literacy, and civic institutions that create forums for public deliberation about the design of national AI systems. It may also demand a cultural shift in which efficiency is no longer treated as the highest good, but balanced against the less quantifiable values of dignity, fairness, and autonomy. To navigate the dilemma requires not the rejection of AI, but its domestication—ensuring that machines remain tools of governance rather than governors in themselves.

The citizen's dilemma, ultimately, is the story of democracy under pressure. Nations may well chart their destinies through code, but whether citizens retain their agency depends on the choices made now about transparency, accountability, and participation. Machine-coded governance does not abolish democracy by fiat; it erodes it through a slow reallocation of decision-making power. To recognise this is to take the first step towards reclaiming agency. For what is at stake is not simply the technical question of how algorithms function, but the political question of who decides the conditions under which they do. *The future of citizenship will be determined by whether individuals accept the passive role of data subjects, or demand their rightful place as co-authors of the algorithmic age.*

Spaces of Resistance

The narrative of artificial intelligence often leans towards inevitability. Systems scale, defaults harden, and societies adapt around them, as if there were no alternative but to accept the encroachment of machine decision-making. Yet inevitability is rarely the whole story of technology. At every moment in history when machinery has threatened to overwhelm human agency, individuals and collectives have carved out spaces of resistance. The algorithmic age is no different. Across courts, parliaments, laboratories, and streets, activists, technologists, and policymakers are working to ensure that the arc of AI bends towards human values rather than away from them. Their actions remind us that while the logic of machines may dominate, it is not destiny.

One of the most visible theatres of resistance lies in the domain of civil liberties. When facial recognition systems began to be rolled out across cities in the United States and Europe, they were initially framed as tools of public safety. Yet studies from institutions such as MIT revealed significant accuracy disparities, with women and people of colour disproportionately misidentified. In response, grassroots organisations like the Algorithmic Justice League, led by computer scientist Joy Buolamwini, mobilised public opinion and pressed for accountability. Their efforts bore fruit: several major US cities, including San Francisco, Boston, and Portland, enacted bans or moratoria on government use of facial recognition. What these victories demonstrate is that resistance does not always require dismantling technology altogether. It can mean imposing democratic guardrails, compelling systems to serve society rather than surveil it. *To resist is to remind governments that the mere availability of a tool does not justify its adoption.*

Legal institutions have also become crucial sites of resistance. The Dutch courts' ruling against SyRI, the welfare fraud detection algorithm, signalled that fundamental rights could not be subordinated to opaque automation. In this case, activists, lawyers, and concerned citizens challenged the state's reliance on black-box analytics, arguing it violated privacy and the European Convention on Human Rights. The decision was significant not only for those directly affected but for its wider principle: states cannot outsource their obligations to protect rights to statistical systems. Similar legal challenges are surfacing elsewhere, from lawsuits against predictive policing in the United States to campaigns contesting automated credit scoring in China. While the outcomes vary, the trend suggests that resistance is increasingly being articulated through law as much as through protest. Courts, long the arena for defining constitutional boundaries, are now being asked to adjudicate on the constitutionality of code.

Policymakers too are shaping spaces where human values can reassert primacy. The European Union's AI Act, currently one of the most ambitious attempts at regulating artificial intelligence, introduces categories of "unacceptable risk" that prohibit certain uses outright, including social scoring. It further imposes stringent obligations on high-risk applications in areas like employment, healthcare, and law enforcement. Although critics argue the regulation is either too heavy-handed or too timid, it nonetheless represents a political assertion that algorithmic governance must operate within democratically determined boundaries. Similar initiatives are emerging in Canada, which has tabled the Artificial Intelligence and Data Act, and in Brazil, which is advancing AI legislation grounded in human rights. These policy efforts are imperfect and contested, but they mark a critical recognition: leaving AI solely to market incentives or geopolitical competition would almost certainly erode human values, not preserve them. *Resistance at the level of lawmaking is an attempt to institutionalise the human voice within the machinery of technological power.*

The role of technologists themselves is equally central. Much of the resistance to unaccountable AI comes from within the institutions building it. Researchers at major firms such as Google and Microsoft have repeatedly sounded alarms about biased datasets, unsafe systems, and irresponsible deployment. The firing of Google researchers Timnit Gebru and Margaret Mitchell in 2020 after raising concerns about large language models sparked a global debate about corporate governance of AI ethics. Their case highlighted the fragility of internal dissent in environments driven by profit and competition, but it also inspired a wave of solidarity and new initiatives outside the corporate sphere. Independent research collectives like Distributed AI Research (DAIR) have since emerged, committed to producing scholarship and advocacy free from corporate capture. This illustrates that technologists, though often employed by powerful firms, are not merely functionaries of technological inevitability. They can, and often do, resist from within, exposing harms and demanding alternative pathways.

What is striking about these spaces of resistance is their diversity. Some are formal and institutional—lawsuits, regulations, oversight bodies. Others are grassroots and improvisational—hacktivist interventions, community campaigns, whistle-blowers. Resistance is not a single movement but a patchwork of efforts that converge on the idea that humans must remain in the loop. Importantly, these efforts are not confined to the West. In Kenya, civil society groups have challenged the government's deployment of biometric ID systems, arguing they exacerbate exclusion for marginalised groups. In India, activists continue to resist the overreach of Aadhaar, particularly in contexts where technical failures block access to essential welfare services. In Latin America, digital rights organisations are contesting surveillance expansions tied to crime prevention. These struggles may not receive the same global attention as debates in Brussels or Washington, but they demonstrate that the defence of human values against algorithmic overreach is a truly global endeavour.

There is, however, a danger in romanticising resistance. Not all efforts succeed, and some are co-opted. Corporate actors increasingly fund "ethics" initiatives and sponsor academic research, raising questions about independence. Policymakers may pass regulations that are broad in ambition but weak in enforcement. Grassroots campaigns may win temporary moratoria that are quietly rolled back when public attention wanes. Resistance must therefore be understood as an ongoing process rather than a definitive victory. *Spaces of resistance are fragile and contingent; their existence depends on constant vigilance and renewal.*

Yet fragility is not weakness. History shows that enduring change often begins with contested, imperfect interventions. Labour rights, civil rights, environmental protections—all were once resisted by powerful economic and political interests, and all were won through persistent struggle. The contest over AI is still in its early stages, but the contours of resistance are already visible. What they share is an insistence that technology be shaped by human values rather than the reverse. That insistence, however modest in the face of powerful forces, is a form of agency in itself.

Ultimately, spaces of resistance serve as reminders that citizens, technologists, and policymakers are not mere passengers on a technological conveyor belt. They can slow it, redirect it, or stop it altogether when it veers into unacceptable territory. They can demand explanation, insist on fairness, and set boundaries. By doing so, they keep alive the essential democratic principle that governance, however mediated by machines, must remain accountable to the people it serves. *Resistance, in its many forms, is the means by which human values stay in the loop—not as a nostalgic afterthought, but as the decisive force shaping the future of national destinies in the age of algorithms.*

Reclaiming the Political

The diffusion of artificial intelligence into the fabric of national governance has quietly shifted the balance of political life. Where decisions once passed through legislatures, bureaucrats, or courts, they are increasingly shaped by code—decisions about welfare eligibility, policing priorities, tax audits, border security, and even resource allocation. The technical rationality of algorithms promises efficiency and objectivity, yet it does so at the cost of transparency, accountability, and human deliberation. Citizens find themselves governed not only by elected officials but also by computational systems whose inner workings are obscure and whose biases may be invisible until harms surface. This is not merely a technological issue; it is a fundamentally political one. *To reclaim the political in the age of AI is to insist that machines serve democratic life rather than supplant it.*

The difficulty lies in the speed and subtlety with which AI colonises decision-making. Consider the rise of predictive policing in American cities. Tools like PredPol were introduced with the promise of data-driven neutrality, only to perpetuate cycles of racial bias by directing more police patrols to historically over-policed neighbourhoods. When challenged, officials often deferred to the authority of the algorithm: the machine, not the human, had determined the outcome. In practice, this deference displaced political responsibility. What should have been a matter of public debate—how resources are distributed, how communities are policed—was presented as a technical inevitability. This displacement illustrates the central danger: AI can convert deeply political choices into questions of technical optimisation, stripping them of their contestable, democratic character.

The same logic has appeared in social welfare systems. In the Netherlands, the SyRI algorithm used to identify potential welfare fraud was struck down by a Dutch court in 2020 for violating human rights, particularly the right to privacy. What the case revealed was not just flawed code but a broader democratic failure. Citizens had little knowledge of how the system worked, no means of challenging decisions, and scant political recourse to demand change. The government had outsourced part of its moral responsibility to an opaque system, and the public only regained its voice through costly litigation. *The lesson is clear: algorithms embedded in governance must not be allowed to obscure political accountability, because what is lost in opacity is not just clarity but democracy itself.*

Calls for transparency and oversight have grown louder in response. In the European Union, the proposed AI Act attempts to categorise systems by risk and impose obligations accordingly. Yet transparency in the AI context is not straightforward. Making source code public does little for most citizens who lack technical expertise. Even experts struggle to interpret the inner workings of large-scale neural networks. Transparency, therefore, must be redefined: not just opening the code but ensuring *comprehensibility*. Citizens need accessible explanations of how systems function, what data they rely on, and how decisions can be challenged. This is less about technical disclosure and more about democratic intelligibility. Without it, the promise of transparency risks becoming an empty ritual, serving institutions more than the public they are meant to protect.

Accountability follows from this. If governments and corporations deploy AI systems that affect fundamental rights, they must be held accountable for the outcomes, not allowed to hide behind the supposed objectivity of code. This principle is being slowly recognised in legal frameworks. The EU's General Data Protection Regulation introduced the "right to explanation," giving individuals the ability to ask how automated decisions affecting them are made. While the right remains limited in practice, it gestures toward a political reassertion of agency. In the United States, debates around Section 230 and platform liability show a growing recognition that digital infrastructures are not neutral but political actors with responsibilities. Accountability requires both legal obligation and cultural expectation: citizens must normalise the demand that when algorithms govern, humans remain answerable.

Human oversight, meanwhile, is often invoked as a safeguard but rarely examined in depth. Too often it is treated as a symbolic checkbox—a human signature on a machine-driven process rather than meaningful review. Genuine oversight requires institutional redesign. It means establishing independent auditing bodies with the authority to inspect algorithms and compel changes. It means embedding ethical review boards into government procurement processes, ensuring that AI systems undergo political scrutiny before adoption. It means training judges, civil servants, and regulators in the basics of algorithmic governance so they cannot be easily blinded by technical jargon. Most importantly, it requires that citizens themselves retain the right to appeal machine-made decisions to human authorities who are both empowered and obligated to intervene. Without such mechanisms, oversight collapses into theatre.

Reclaiming the political also means grappling with the tension between national sovereignty and global AI development. The largest AI systems are developed by a handful of corporations spanning the United States and China, raising the question of how smaller nations can demand accountability from technologies not built within their borders. One response is international cooperation: the OECD's AI principles, UNESCO's ethical guidelines, and the G7's discussions on trustworthy AI attempt to set cross-border standards. Yet global frameworks risk dilution, producing lowest-common-denominator commitments without teeth. National governments must still cultivate the capacity to regulate within their borders and resist the narrative that technological competition requires sacrificing democratic values. *The demand for oversight is not parochial but planetary; still, its enforcement must begin locally, where citizens can exert direct pressure.*

Examples of citizen mobilisation already show how the political can be reclaimed. In Toronto, public backlash forced Sidewalk Labs, a subsidiary of Alphabet, to abandon its plan for a data-driven "smart city" after concerns about surveillance and data ownership. In South Korea, student protests challenged the use of AI-based university admissions systems that were found to entrench inequality. These cases underscore that when citizens refuse to accept AI as inevitable, they can reshape its trajectory. Resistance is not merely symbolic; it can reorient policy and constrain corporate ambition. *Democracy in the age of AI will depend on citizens remembering that technology is always contestable, and contestation is a political right, not a technical inconvenience.*

Yet the struggle is uneven. In authoritarian regimes, AI is often deployed as a tool of surveillance and control, from China's social credit system to Russia's facial recognition cameras monitoring protests. Here, reclaiming the political takes on a more dangerous form, where resistance risks imprisonment or worse. Even so, activists persist, using VPNs, encryption, and alternative networks to carve out fragile spaces of autonomy. These contexts remind us that transparency and oversight are not luxuries but essentials. Where they are absent, technology becomes an extension of state power unchecked by democratic consent. For democratic nations, the warning is stark: fail to embed oversight now, and systems will calcify in ways that are difficult to reverse.

The central challenge, then, is cultural as much as institutional. Citizens must re-learn to see technology as political, rather than as neutral infrastructure. The internet was once treated as a sphere beyond politics, only to reveal itself as deeply entangled with power. AI is repeating the pattern. To resist this drift, political education must evolve. Universities, civic groups, and media must help foster literacy not just in how AI works but in how it governs. *Political imagination must expand to include the algorithm as a site of power, and therefore a site of contestation.* Without such a shift, citizens risk becoming passive recipients of machine-mediated governance, unable to reclaim the authority that democracy promises.

Ultimately, reclaiming the political in the age of AI is about more than transparency, accountability, and oversight—it is about the preservation of citizenship itself. If national destinies are increasingly coded into systems designed by engineers, influenced by corporate incentives, and deployed by governments seeking efficiency, then the task of citizens is to reassert their collective right to shape those choices. The machinery of politics cannot be allowed to dissolve into the machinery of code. To accept such a dissolution would be to concede that democracy was an interlude rather than a foundation. The political is not given; it must be reclaimed, again and again, wherever machines begin to rule.

Chapter 10

The Future Is Already Unevenly Distributed

The story of artificial intelligence has already slipped beyond the confines of laboratories and start-ups, insinuating itself into the structures of state power, economic competition, and everyday life. Yet what is striking is not simply its reach, but its unevenness. Some nations are shaping global architectures of influence through vast computational infrastructures, while others struggle to maintain even minimal sovereignty in a world where algorithmic capacity is rapidly becoming the determinant of power. The landscape of AI is fractured, its benefits and risks distributed asymmetrically, and its trajectory contested by actors with vastly divergent interests. Unlike earlier technological revolutions, the politics of AI cannot be neatly disentangled from its technical development; each advance in modelling scale, each refinement of data processing, reshapes the hierarchy of nations. To speak of AI as merely another disruptive technology is therefore to miss the scale of its implications. It is less a tool than a force that reconfigures sovereignty itself.

History offers a partial lens through which to view this shift. When nuclear weapons emerged in the mid-twentieth century, they too redefined global order. The bomb was not just another instrument of war but a threshold technology that altered the calculus of state survival, forcing adversaries into a fragile equilibrium underpinned by deterrence. Arms control treaties, verification regimes, and international institutions became essential scaffolding to prevent catastrophe. There is a temptation, then, to reach for nuclear history as a template for AI governance. Yet the comparison both illuminates and misleads. Nuclear weapons were discrete, scarce, and spectacularly destructive, making their spread both visible and, to some degree, containable. AI, by contrast, is diffuse, dual-use, and woven into civilian as much as military infrastructures. Its power derives not from a single device but from networks of data, computation, and algorithms that proliferate across borders. Regulating such a system is vastly more complex. Where nuclear arms control involved counting warheads and monitoring enrichment sites, AI governance must grapple with invisible lines of code, models updated overnight, and the commercial incentives of trillion-dollar corporations. The very conditions that enabled nuclear treaties—the clarity of the threat, the limited number of actors, the visibility of production—are absent here. The lesson from nuclear history, then, is not that regulation is impossible, but that the mechanisms of global order must adapt to a technology that resists containment by design.

If AI cannot be corralled within the frameworks that governed nuclear weapons, then what futures are plausibly ahead? One possibility is the consolidation of an AI super-empire, where a handful of states, led by the United States and China, dominate not only the technological frontier but the terms of political and economic engagement for the rest of the world. Smaller nations in this scenario would find themselves as digital client states, dependent on the infrastructures, platforms, and standards dictated by hegemonic powers. The asymmetry of access to frontier models would reinforce global inequalities, with data sovereignty ceded in exchange for access to services. Another possibility is fragmentation, with nations clustering into algorithmic blocs. Much as the Cold War saw competing economic and ideological systems, the AI age could splinter into incompatible technological spheres, with separate standards for data governance, surveillance, and digital commerce. Europe's emphasis on rights-based regulation, China's state-driven control, and America's market-led dynamism already hint at such divergence. The final scenario is more aspirational: a negotiated algorithmic commons, where nations, corporations, and civil society develop shared frameworks to govern AI as a planetary infrastructure. Here, mechanisms of transparency, accountability, and equitable access would be embedded in global institutions, not merely national strategies. Yet such a commons requires unprecedented levels of trust and cooperation in a geopolitical environment defined by rivalry.

The difficulty lies in the fragile middle path. Establishing global governance mechanisms for AI is not an abstract ideal but a necessity if the technology is to be steered towards collective benefit rather than domination. Yet the very conditions of the international system—mistrust between rival powers, competing economic incentives, asymmetries in technical capability—militate against such cooperation. Even when agreements are struck, as with climate accords, enforcement remains tenuous, undermined by national interests. In the case of AI, where strategic advantage is perceived to hinge on being first, the incentives to defect are enormous. No great power is eager to bind itself with rules that might constrain its capacity to deploy advanced systems for intelligence, warfare, or economic advantage. The fragile middle path, then, is not a compromise readily achieved but a tightrope walk between the collapse into digital empires and the hope of cooperative stewardship. To sustain it requires more than diplomacy; it demands rethinking sovereignty in terms of shared risks and mutual interdependence.

For readers seeking clarity amidst these possibilities, a final framework is necessary—one that shifts the conversation beyond technical breakthroughs or policy proposals to the deeper question of what AI represents for the future of political order. AI should be understood not only as a technology but as a determinant of sovereignty, order, and survival. Its deployment determines which nations hold leverage in international affairs, which societies enjoy resilience or vulnerability, and which values are encoded into the architectures that shape human life. Sovereignty in this sense is no longer defined only by control of territory or resources, but by control of data flows, computational infrastructures, and algorithmic systems that decide how populations are governed. Order is no longer a matter of military balance or institutional treaties alone, but of aligning the standards, protocols, and norms that structure the digital world. Survival itself may hinge not only on deterring hostile actors but on ensuring that AI does not entrench catastrophic risks—from autonomous weapons spiralling beyond control to economic systems destabilised by machine-driven speculation.

The uneven distribution of AI futures is already visible. Wealthy nations build large language models that rival the scale of natural ecosystems, while poorer states struggle to digitise basic services. Corporations with server farms spanning continents dictate the pace of innovation, while governments scramble to retrofit regulatory frameworks. Citizens in some jurisdictions enjoy rights to appeal algorithmic decisions, while others are subject to unaccountable machine verdicts. This asymmetry is not incidental; it is the structure of the present. The challenge of the coming decades is whether humanity can transform this unevenness into a more just and sustainable order, or whether it will calcify into a hierarchy as enduring as the global nuclear order of the Cold War. The future may already be distributed unevenly, but it remains within the grasp of politics, imagination, and struggle to determine how permanent that distribution will be.

The chapter that follows does not attempt to predict which path will prevail. Rather, it offers tools for thinking: lessons drawn from history, scenarios that illuminate the range of plausible futures, and frameworks that help disentangle the stakes. The point is not to provide closure but to equip readers with the clarity to see AI for what it is—not merely a collection of algorithms, but a reordering of the human condition on which sovereignty, order, and survival now depend.

Lessons From Nuclear History

The detonation of the first atomic bomb in 1945 created a stark recognition: humanity had entered an age where a single technology could determine the fate of civilisation. States scrambled not only to acquire nuclear capability but also to contain its use, producing an unprecedented architecture of treaties, monitoring regimes, and diplomatic frameworks. This history has become a touchstone for thinking about artificial intelligence. Yet while the nuclear past offers cautionary lessons, it also underlines why AI presents a regulatory challenge of a wholly different order. Comparing the two illuminates both the possibility of learning from history and the limits of analogy in addressing an emerging technology whose reach is less visible, more pervasive, and harder to contain.

Nuclear weapons were singular in their destructiveness and relatively easy to count. An intercontinental ballistic missile launch could be tracked from satellites, a reactor could be monitored for uranium enrichment, and a warhead could be dismantled in a verifiable process. These material properties made it possible to construct agreements such as the Strategic Arms Limitation Talks (SALT), the Non-Proliferation Treaty (NPT), and the later Strategic Arms Reduction Treaty (START), which hinged on the ability of adversaries to trust verification mechanisms. Artificial intelligence, by contrast, leaves no mushroom cloud and requires no enriched uranium. A large language model can be replicated with sufficient computing power, its training data dispersed across cloud servers, and its upgrades rolled out in software updates invisible to outsiders. The very attributes that made nuclear regulation feasible—the discreteness of the technology, the concentration of expertise, the visibility of use—are largely absent in the domain of AI.

The differences are stark, but so too are the echoes. Just as nuclear breakthroughs initially occurred in secret, with the Manhattan Project cloaked in wartime urgency, so too are the most powerful AI systems today concentrated within a small set of actors—predominantly American and Chinese technology firms, supported by state-level investment. In both cases, the frontier is controlled by elites with disproportionate influence over global security. The Cold War nuclear order was characterised by the tension between secrecy and disclosure: how much could adversaries reveal to build trust without compromising advantage? AI is developing under similar dynamics. Firms speak of transparency and ethical safeguards while guarding proprietary algorithms and data sets that constitute their competitive edge. *Opacity, then as now, is both a strategic resource and a global risk.*

Another instructive parallel lies in the dual-use nature of both technologies. Nuclear fission produced both the bomb and the reactor, both annihilation and electricity. Artificial intelligence likewise powers medical diagnostics, climate modelling, and financial systems while simultaneously enabling autonomous weapons, surveillance regimes, and disinformation at scale. The challenge for regulation is not distinguishing military from civilian use—the line is blurred beyond recognition—but managing a spectrum of applications whose impact depends less on their technical form than on their political context. In nuclear history, the peaceful atom could never be entirely separated from the martial one. The same truth applies to AI: tools for language translation can become engines of propaganda; image recognition can serve both healthcare and authoritarian surveillance.

Despite these parallels, the global political environment differs in ways that complicate governance. Nuclear arms control unfolded in a bipolar system where the United States and the Soviet Union dominated. Their rivalry was intense, but the limited number of actors made agreements conceivable. Today's AI landscape is multipolar. Alongside the United States and China, the European Union asserts regulatory leadership, middle powers like India and South Korea invest heavily in AI strategies, and private corporations hold capacities that rival or exceed those of states. Unlike nuclear physics, which was firmly embedded in state-led military-industrial complexes, AI's leading edge is shaped by private enterprise motivated as much by shareholder value as national security. Regulation, then, is not merely a matter of international treaties between governments but also of constraining corporate power—an arena where traditional arms control mechanisms have little precedent.

The impossibility of directly transplanting nuclear frameworks into AI becomes clearest when considering verification. Nuclear treaties relied on inspection: satellite imagery, on-site visits, and technical monitoring of fissile material. These provided confidence that commitments were being honoured. By contrast, AI progress is measured in abstract parameters—training runs, model weights, proprietary data sets—most of which can be concealed within private infrastructures. A nation could sign an

AI treaty while continuing to develop cutting-edge models in hidden facilities, shielded by corporate confidentiality and the ease of distributing computational tasks across jurisdictions. The very qualities that make AI flexible and dynamic also render it resistant to conventional forms of verification. *If nuclear arms control was predicated on visibility, AI governance confronts the challenge of invisibility.*

Yet it would be misleading to suggest that nuclear history has nothing to teach. One key lesson is that existential risk can force adversaries to negotiate even under deep mistrust. The Cuban Missile Crisis demonstrated that the logic of deterrence could bring humanity to the brink of annihilation, compelling both superpowers to establish hotlines and pursue treaties they might otherwise have resisted. The analogy for AI is imperfect, but instructive: only when catastrophic scenarios become undeniable—autonomous weapons misfiring in conflict, or runaway systems causing economic chaos—might the political will for global governance emerge. Nuclear history warns that regulation is often reactive, born from crisis rather than foresight. If AI governance follows this pattern, the world may endure significant harm before serious mechanisms are in place.

There is also a subtler lesson in how norms were constructed. Long before treaties were signed, cultural taboos around nuclear use began to crystallise. The horror of Hiroshima and Nagasaki created a global sentiment that nuclear war was morally unacceptable, even when technically feasible. Over time, this taboo became a restraint in itself. For AI, a comparable process is underway: debates about algorithmic fairness, human oversight, and the ethics of autonomous systems are slowly shaping a moral horizon. Though not enforceable in the way treaties are, such norms can influence behaviour, deterring reckless deployment and providing the groundwork for future regulation. *Where formal verification fails, normative power may fill the gap.*

Nevertheless, the limits of analogy must be acknowledged. Nuclear technology stabilised into a relatively narrow set of applications: weapons and reactors. Artificial intelligence, by contrast, is open-ended, generative, and perpetually evolving. Its trajectory is shaped not only by statecraft but by consumer markets, research communities, and cross-border networks of innovation. Containment in the nuclear sense is therefore impossible; AI cannot be "frozen" at a given stage of development. Attempting to regulate it as if it were a bounded technology risks misunderstanding its dynamism. The challenge is not preventing proliferation—AI is already proliferating—

but shaping its integration into societies in ways that preserve human agency and prevent catastrophic misuse.

What, then, is the truest lesson from nuclear history? Perhaps it is this: existential technologies force humanity to confront the inadequacy of existing political structures. The United Nations was never designed for nuclear arms control, yet it became a forum for negotiating non-proliferation. Similarly, today's patchwork of national regulations and voluntary guidelines is insufficient for AI. What is required is not the replication of past institutions but the creation of new ones attuned to the realities of digital infrastructure, corporate power, and rapid innovation. Nuclear arms control shows that governance is possible under conditions of rivalry, but it also highlights that the nature of the technology dictates the form of the governance.

To compare nuclear weapons and artificial intelligence is therefore to hold a mirror to the changing nature of global order. One was a material object, scarce and terrifyingly visible; the other is a distributed system, invisible yet omnipresent. One lent itself to treaties defined by counting and monitoring; the other defies such measures, demanding instead novel approaches grounded in transparency, ethics, and adaptive oversight. The similarities underscore the stakes; the differences reveal the unprecedented challenge. If nuclear history tells us anything, it is that ignoring the risks until catastrophe strikes is the most dangerous path of all.

Possible Futures

The global contest over artificial intelligence is not merely about technology but about the architecture of world order. Just as the industrial revolution reordered societies and nuclear weapons reshaped geopolitics, advanced AI is creating the conditions for new political realities. The question is not whether AI will transform the balance of power, but which form that transformation will take. Three plausible futures are already visible on the horizon: the dominance of a single AI super-empire, the hardening of fragmented algorithmic blocs, or the negotiation of an algorithmic commons that resembles shared governance. Each scenario is shaped by history, economics, and human ambition, and each carries profound consequences for sovereignty and survival.

The first scenario—an AI super-empire—is in many ways the most intuitive. History shows that technologies with steep barriers to entry often produce hierarchies of power. Nuclear weapons were monopolised for decades by a handful of states, and even today remain concentrated in the hands of a few. AI, while less tangible, is already moving in a similar direction: the most advanced models are trained on massive computational clusters, requiring specialised hardware, scarce talent, and energy resources so large that only a small number of corporations and governments can realistically build them. If the United States, China, or even a transnational consortium of corporate actors manage to establish a decisive lead—one that is technologically and economically insurmountable—they could emerge as the central authority in a unipolar AI order.

Such a super-empire would hold disproportionate sway over military capabilities, financial infrastructures, and information ecosystems. Control of frontier AI systems would enable it to outpace rivals in scientific discovery, economic growth, and intelligence gathering. *The entity at the apex would not merely dominate markets; it would shape the very parameters of global decision-making.* For weaker states, this would mean a profound loss of autonomy, as national strategies would need to be calibrated against the interests of the AI hegemon. Some might welcome this concentration, imagining that a single steward could ensure coherence and prevent reckless proliferation. Yet the dangers are obvious: monopolised AI power risks entrenching authoritarian governance, suppressing dissent, and locking the world into a form of digital dependency. Just as nuclear dominance fuelled decades of strategic fear, so too would AI supremacy likely generate cycles of resistance and counterforce.

The second scenario—fragmented algorithmic blocs—may in fact be more consistent with the world's current trajectory. Instead of a single dominant power, competing centres of AI development could consolidate around geopolitical, cultural, or economic alignments. Much as the Cold War produced NATO and the Warsaw Pact, or as today's internet infrastructure divides along Western, Chinese, and increasingly regionalised lines, AI ecosystems could calcify into blocs defined by standards, governance frameworks, and supply chain dependencies. Already the European Union is attempting to establish its own regulatory vision, framing AI as a matter of rights and ethics rather than sheer scale of performance. India has articulated ambitions for AI sovereignty, wary of dependence on either Washington or Beijing. Africa, long marginalised in previous technological waves, has begun advocating for inclusion in shaping AI governance. These moves suggest that rather than coalescing into a single order, AI may harden into rival spheres.

Fragmentation carries its own logic. States and corporations may prefer to control their own models, their own data sets, and their own cloud infrastructures rather than accept dependence on external suppliers. The rise of national AI strategies illustrates this impulse towards autonomy. In practice, this would mean not only competing AI systems but competing algorithmic values: one bloc might prioritise state-led surveillance, another individual privacy; one might optimise for military dominance, another for human-centred design. The world would be less about one empire than about contested algorithmic sovereignties. *Global interdependence would still exist—no bloc could cut itself off entirely—but the rules of interaction would be governed by rivalry rather than shared vision.*

This scenario has precedent in technological history. The early days of the internet promised a borderless commons, but it soon fractured into nationally controlled networks. Semiconductor supply chains, once highly integrated, are now being decoupled along security lines. AI, too, may succumb to the same centrifugal forces. For citizens, this would mean divergent experiences of technology: different languages of interaction, different rights to privacy, different vulnerabilities to manipulation. For states, it would mean navigating a multipolar competition where technological alignment becomes as important as military alliance. Fragmentation would likely reduce the risks of a single hegemon dictating terms, but it would also raise the probability of miscalculation, escalation, and technological arms races.

The third scenario—the negotiated algorithmic commons—presents the most difficult yet arguably the most desirable path. It imagines a world in which states, corporations, and civil societies recognise that AI, like the atmosphere or the oceans, is a shared domain whose misuse could imperil all. In such a future, instead of racing to dominate or entrench, the major actors would establish cooperative frameworks: global treaties on autonomous weapons, transparent standards for safety testing, shared repositories for high-risk applications, and international oversight bodies capable of intervening in moments of crisis. Just as the Law of the Sea or the Paris Climate Agreement attempted to govern shared spaces, so too could an algorithmic commons provide guardrails for a technology whose risks are not confined by borders.

This vision may sound utopian, but its necessity is becoming harder to deny. Autonomous weapons deployed without oversight could destabilise entire regions; algorithmic disinformation could corrode democratic institutions; unchecked concentration of AI power could create systemic economic inequality. *No single actor, however powerful, can fully insulate itself from these risks.* The commons approach recognises this interdependence and seeks to channel competition into frameworks that prevent catastrophe. Real-world experiments already hint at its feasibility. The Partnership on AI brings together companies and NGOs to establish ethical best practices. UNESCO has produced a global recommendation on the ethics of AI, signed by nearly 200 countries. These may be embryonic steps, but they point towards the idea that governance is possible when enough actors acknowledge the stakes.

Yet the difficulty of sustaining a commons must not be underestimated. Unlike climate or nuclear governance, AI lacks a clear physical metric for monitoring compliance. States will hesitate to reveal their capabilities, fearing espionage or disadvantage. Corporations will resist regulation that limits profitability. Civil society, though increasingly vocal, struggles to match the lobbying power of industry giants. The challenge, then, is not recognising the need for an algorithmic commons but creating mechanisms strong enough to resist the gravitational pull of rivalry and monopoly. History suggests that only crises generate such cooperation: nuclear arms control emerged after near-catastrophe; climate agreements gained traction only after decades of visible environmental damage. If AI follows this pattern, the commons may be negotiated only after a profound failure reveals the inadequacy of fragmented or hegemonic orders.

The three scenarios—super-empire, blocs, commons—are not mutually exclusive. They may unfold sequentially or even coexist in hybrid forms. A dominant actor may emerge temporarily, only to face counter-balancing coalitions that create blocs. Out of exhaustion or fear, these blocs may eventually negotiate shared frameworks that resemble a commons. Alternatively, the world may remain stuck in a cycle of rivalry without ever reaching the cooperative stage. *The decisive factor will be whether political imagination can keep pace with technological acceleration.* The longer governance lags, the more likely the future will be defined by either monopoly or fragmentation rather than by a negotiated settlement.

Thinking through these scenarios is not an exercise in speculation but a tool for clarity. They remind us that AI is not an abstract force but a determinant of sovereignty, order, and survival. Each pathway has precedents, each carries risks, and each demands choices by governments, corporations, and citizens. The future is not preordained; it will be shaped by the distribution of power, the willingness to cooperate, and the recognition of shared vulnerability. Whether we live under the shadow of an empire, within rival blocs, or inside a fragile commons will depend less on the algorithms themselves than on the political decisions surrounding them. *AI may be technological in form, but it is political in destiny.*

The Fragile Middle Path

The ambition to establish global governance for artificial intelligence often rests on an assumption that the international community, faced with sufficient risk, will find the collective will to cooperate. History, however, offers sobering reminders of how rarely such coordination emerges. Even nuclear weapons—whose catastrophic potential was visible within days of their first use—have never been fully placed under supranational control. Climate change, another existential challenge with clear scientific consensus, has seen decades of pledges that falter against the friction of national self-interest. AI sits uneasily between these precedents: unlike nuclear technology it is decentralised, adaptive, and embedded in civilian economies, yet like climate change its effects are diffuse, cumulative, and global. The middle path of shared governance is possible, but it is fragile precisely because the incentives to diverge are greater than the incentives to converge.

The fragility begins with the asymmetry of capabilities. A small handful of states and corporations possess the resources to develop frontier AI systems, while most of the world is a consumer rather than a producer of these technologies. The promise of governance must therefore navigate a stark power imbalance: those who lead in AI development have little desire to restrict their own advantage, and those left behind struggle to gain a seat at the negotiating table. Consider the early debates over nuclear non-proliferation. The United States and the Soviet Union argued for restrictions only after they had secured their arsenals; their commitments were structured to preserve dominance, not to yield it. Today's AI leaders, whether in Silicon Valley, Shenzhen, or elsewhere, have every incentive to replicate this pattern by shaping governance frameworks that entrench their primacy. This dynamic makes the prospect of equitable global rules tenuous, as weaker states suspect that "universal" standards are in fact instruments of hierarchy.

Moreover, AI's pervasiveness across economic and social life complicates any attempt at shared control. Nuclear weapons could be cordoned off as a military issue; climate change, though far-reaching, is anchored in measurable emissions. AI resists such neat containment. A system trained for medical diagnostics may also inform surveillance; an algorithm built for logistics optimisation may be adapted for military supply chains.

Governance, in this context, cannot draw clean lines between permissible and impermissible uses. Instead, it must contend with technologies whose applications mutate rapidly and whose impacts blur across domains. *This fluidity undermines the very idea of enforceable treaties.* How does one verify compliance when the same model can be repurposed in secret? How does one legislate when the boundaries between civilian benefit and strategic threat are porous?

Diverging political values further erode the possibility of a stable middle path. Democracies tend to emphasise transparency, accountability, and rights, while authoritarian states privilege state control, security, and efficiency. Attempts to draft global AI principles immediately confront these value divides. The European Union's regulatory framework reflects a rights-based tradition, while China's governance emphasises order and stability. Both may use the language of safety, but their interpretations diverge fundamentally. This is not simply a matter of misaligned incentives but of incompatible philosophical premises. To establish shared rules under such conditions would require unprecedented compromise, yet the political realities of great power rivalry discourage concession. If a governance framework threatens to constrain one bloc's preferred values, it will be rejected or hollowed out. Thus, what emerges instead are declarations of intent, thin agreements that leave ample space for unilateral interpretation.

The private sector introduces an additional layer of complexity. Unlike nuclear or climate governance, where states are the primary actors, AI development is driven by corporations whose resources outstrip those of many governments. Companies such as OpenAI, DeepMind, or Baidu sit at the frontier of research and wield influence over deployment decisions with global consequences. This dispersal of power across public and private spheres makes the governance problem qualitatively different. States can sign treaties, but they cannot easily bind corporations that operate across jurisdictions and pursue profit motives that may conflict with safety. Corporate self-regulation codes of ethics, voluntary reporting—offers little reassurance given the competitive pressures of the market. *The fragile middle path, then, must contend with governance structures that cannot rest on state sovereignty alone but require unprecedented mechanisms of public-private coordination.*

Even where cooperation emerges, fragility is evident in enforcement. The Paris Climate Agreement demonstrates how international accords often rely on voluntary compliance, peer pressure, and reputational costs rather than binding sanctions. AI governance risks reproducing this weakness.

Verification is technically challenging, monitoring is politically sensitive, and penalties are difficult to apply against powerful states or corporations. The likely outcome is a regime of soft norms—principles of safety, fairness, and transparency—that are cited frequently but enforced inconsistently. Such norms may shape behaviour at the margins, but they lack the robustness required to manage high-stakes risks. The middle path thus risks becoming not a true governance mechanism but a symbolic gesture that masks ongoing divergence.

Yet one must not dismiss fragility as futility. Fragile structures, though easily broken, can nonetheless provide scaffolding for more resilient arrangements. Consider the Nuclear Non-Proliferation Treaty: criticised for its hypocrisy, riddled with loopholes, yet still effective in limiting the spread of nuclear weapons beyond a small group of states. Imperfect governance can buy time, create forums for dialogue, and establish precedents that later strengthen. In AI, a fragile middle path could take the form of global agreements on narrow issues—prohibitions on autonomous nuclear launch systems, mandatory safety evaluations for frontier models, or shared incident reporting mechanisms. While insufficient to regulate AI comprehensively, such measures could reduce immediate risks and provide foundations for more ambitious cooperation should crises escalate. *Fragility does not eliminate value; it defines the limits within which value must be carefully cultivated.*

A further dimension of fragility arises from public trust. Governance regimes require legitimacy, and legitimacy rests on the perception that rules serve the collective rather than a privileged minority. If citizens perceive AI governance as elite manipulation—whether by dominant states or corporations—the legitimacy of any framework collapses. The history of global trade institutions illustrates this risk: once celebrated as engines of shared prosperity, they became targets of backlash when inequalities widened. AI governance faces the same danger. The middle path will fracture unless it demonstrates not only technical safety but distributive fairness: that the benefits of AI are not captured exclusively by those already powerful, and that safeguards extend to vulnerable populations who might otherwise be excluded.

The fragility of the middle path, then, is not a single problem but a constellation of tensions: between powerful and weak states, between competing values, between public and private actors, between symbolic commitments and enforceable rules, between elite negotiations and mass legitimacy. Each tension pulls against the possibility of durable governance, and together they create a precarious equilibrium that may hold only under favourable conditions. *The middle path is less a stable road than a tightrope stretched across divergent interests, navigable only with constant adjustment and vigilance.*

Recognising fragility does not mean abandoning the pursuit of global governance. It means acknowledging that success will look less like a grand treaty and more like a patchwork of partial, evolving, and imperfect arrangements. The world is unlikely to produce a single governing authority for AI; it may, however, generate overlapping agreements, regional frameworks, and coalitions of the willing that collectively approximate restraint. The task of statesmen, corporations, and citizens alike is to nurture these fragile structures without expecting them to solve all problems at once. Survival may depend not on perfect governance but on the resilience of fragile mechanisms to adapt under stress.

If history is any guide, the fragility of governance is not a passing inconvenience but a permanent condition of international life. Nuclear weapons were never fully tamed, climate change has never been decisively arrested, and AI will likely elude comprehensive regulation. Yet in each case, even fragile efforts altered the trajectory of risk. They slowed arms races, encouraged innovation in clean energy, and may yet constrain the reckless deployment of powerful algorithms. The fragile middle path for AI governance will be no different: vulnerable, contested, and perpetually incomplete, yet indispensable as the only alternative to unrestrained competition or hegemonic control. *The challenge is not to overcome fragility but to learn how to govern through it.*

A Framework for Clarity

The debate about artificial intelligence often collapses into a familiar rhythm of technical marvels, economic forecasts, and dystopian warnings. Yet framing AI in terms of applications or hazards misses its deeper significance: *it is not simply a tool but a determinant of sovereignty, order, and survival.* To think of AI merely as another technology is to misunderstand its structural role in shaping the capacity of states, the balance of global power, and the rules that govern collective life. Just as the industrial revolution defined the competitive advantages of the nineteenth century and nuclear capability redefined the calculus of deterrence in the twentieth, mastery of advanced algorithms now serves as the organising principle of the twenty-first century. To understand AI with clarity is to place it within this lineage of power-defining transformations rather than treating it as a passing wave of innovation.

The first dimension of this framework lies in sovereignty. Sovereignty is no longer secured solely by territorial control or conventional military force but by the ability to command digital infrastructures, control flows of data, and ensure autonomy in the creation and deployment of algorithmic systems. A country that relies entirely on foreign firms for its AI capabilities is in effect outsourcing a core element of its sovereignty, much as dependence on foreign oil once constrained national policy. This dependency can manifest in subtle but far-reaching ways: vulnerability to supply chain disruptions in semiconductors, exposure to manipulation through algorithmic disinformation, or loss of competitive advantage in industries where AI-enhanced productivity sets the pace of growth. Sovereignty in the AI age is therefore not a static legal claim but a dynamic capacity, measured by the degree to which states can *design, adapt, and safeguard* algorithmic systems without being beholden to external powers.

Order, the second pillar of the framework, refers to the arrangements—formal and informal—that regulate relations among states and societies. Throughout history, new technologies have destabilised existing orders by redistributing power. The advent of gunpowder eroded feudal hierarchies; the telegraph reshaped empire by compressing distance; nuclear weapons froze major power wars under the shadow of mutually assured destruction. AI introduces a different kind of disruption: it creates asymmetries not only in military power but in governance capacity itself. States with advanced AI can monitor populations more effectively, predict economic shifts more accurately, and manipulate information ecosystems more persuasively than those without. This widens the gap between order-makers and order-takers. The international system becomes less a multipolar balance than an algorithmically stratified hierarchy. Understanding AI as an ordering force means recognising that debates about its ethics or safety are inseparable from struggles over who sets the rules and whose interests those rules reflect.

Survival, the third element, extends beyond the existential risk narratives of superintelligence. It is about the resilience of societies under conditions where AI mediates everything from critical infrastructure to food supply chains. A disruption in AI-enabled logistics could paralyse global trade; a cyberattack leveraging generative AI could collapse trust in financial systems; an error in autonomous defence systems could escalate into armed conflict. Survival also concerns the adaptability of political institutions. Democracies, for example, face the challenge of integrating algorithmic governance without hollowing out deliberative processes, while authoritarian states confront the paradox of using AI to centralise control even as it accelerates social and economic complexity that resists centralisation. *The measure of survival in the AI era is not only whether humanity avoids catastrophe but whether political and social systems retain the capacity to absorb shocks and preserve legitimacy under algorithmic pressures.*

When woven together, these three strands—sovereignty, order, survival—form a model that clarifies AI's role as a structuring condition of geopolitics. This model helps cut through the noise of overblown hype on the one hand and complacent minimisation on the other. It grounds the discussion in the recognition that AI functions simultaneously at three levels: as an asset that nations seek to secure, as a system that shapes global hierarchy, and as a force that determines whether institutions can withstand disruption. Each level interacts with the others. A state that loses sovereignty in AI development risks exclusion from shaping global order; exclusion from global order diminishes its resilience; diminished resilience, in turn, erodes sovereignty further. *The clarity lies in understanding these dynamics not as parallel challenges but as interlocking conditions that define the prospects of nations and humanity as a whole.*

To illustrate this framework concretely, consider the example of semiconductor supply chains. Sovereignty is compromised when states lack control over chip fabrication, as advanced AI requires processors manufactured by a handful of firms in Taiwan, South Korea, and the United States. Order is affected because these supply chains become strategic chokepoints, with export controls weaponised to determine who can participate in the frontier of AI development. Survival enters the picture because disruptions—whether from geopolitical conflict, natural disaster, or industrial sabotage—could paralyse AI-dependent systems worldwide. A single domain, semiconductors, thus reveals how sovereignty, order, and survival converge in the politics of AI.

This framework also clarifies the limitations of current debates. Calls for ethical AI, for example, often assume that shared values can be articulated in universal codes. Yet without addressing sovereignty, these codes risk being imposed by the powerful on the weak. Similarly, discussions of global AI governance frequently invoke analogies to arms control, but they neglect how order in the nuclear age rested on the clear visibility of deterrence; by contrast, the opacity of algorithms makes verification difficult and trust elusive. Even the discourse on existential risk tends to focus narrowly on hypothetical future superintelligence, overlooking how survival is already threatened by algorithmic systems embedded in fragile infrastructures today. By reorienting analysis through sovereignty, order, and survival, the framework not only organises the problem space but corrects distortions that arise when AI is treated in isolation from geopolitical realities.

Philosophically, the framework underscores a sobering truth: technologies that redefine sovereignty, order, and survival are never neutral. They are not passive tools awaiting ethical use; they are structuring conditions that shape what is possible, permissible, and inevitable in political life. Just as the logic of nuclear deterrence constrained strategy regardless of leaders' intentions, the logic of algorithmic dependency constrains how societies can act. For example, reliance on AI for managing critical infrastructure creates incentives to prioritise stability over transparency, efficiency over participation, centralisation over decentralisation. Recognising this determinative quality does not absolve human agency but situates it within the boundaries of technological structuring. *Clarity requires acknowledging that AI is not a realm of choice unbounded but of choices already conditioned by the systems we have built.*

The framework also invites a shift in how we imagine possible futures. Instead of debating whether AI will be "good" or "bad," it directs attention to how different distributions of sovereignty, different architectures of order, and different thresholds of survival resilience will shape global trajectories. An AI "super-empire" scenario, where one state or bloc achieves decisive advantage, is intelligible through this model as the concentration of sovereignty leading to an imposed order and fragile survival for all others. A fragmented world of competing algorithmic blocs reflects contested sovereignty, unstable order, and heightened risks to survival from miscalculation. A negotiated commons, by contrast, would be one where sovereignty is partially pooled, order is stabilised through institutional compromise, and survival is bolstered by shared safeguards. The value of the framework is not in predicting which scenario will prevail but in equipping decision-makers to assess which levers they can realistically move within each dimension.

Clarity is not an end-state but a compass. By seeing AI as a determinant of sovereignty, order, and survival, we avoid the twin errors of treating it as a narrow technical problem or as a mystical force beyond comprehension. We place it where it belongs: at the heart of the structures that govern power and possibility. This perspective enables policymakers, business leaders, and citizens alike to evaluate trade-offs with greater realism. Should a nation sacrifice some economic efficiency to preserve AI sovereignty? Should societies accept less transparency in order to maintain algorithmic stability in critical systems? Should international institutions prioritise order even at the cost of fairness? These are not abstract questions but immediate dilemmas whose resolution will shape the trajectory of this century.

The task ahead is not to tame AI as one might tame a wild invention but to understand it as the terrain upon which politics now unfolds. Sovereignty, order, and survival are not optional frames but the coordinates by which states and societies will navigate the age of algorithms. *To see AI clearly is to grasp that our future legitimacy, stability, and endurance are inseparable from how we manage this determinant of collective life.* The framework offers no comforting blueprint, but it does provide the necessary clarity: AI is not one issue among many but the axis around which questions of power and survival now turn.

About the Author

Arden Hale is a writer and strategist who studies how emerging technologies reorder power between states, markets, and citizens. For more than a decade, Hale has worked at the intersection of AI policy, semiconductor supply chains, and digital governance, translating complex research into decision-ready insights for leaders in business and public life. Hale's work blends historical perspective with systems thinking and a practical question that runs through every page: who gains when code becomes law? Empire of Algorithms continues this inquiry—offering a clear, grounded framework for readers who want to understand, and responsibly shape, the rules of the coming order.

www.ingramcontent.com/pod-product-compliance
Lightning Source LLC
Chambersburg PA
CBHW021215250926
51852CB00006B/24
* 9 7 8 9 3 9 0 3 4 9 4 3 2 *